How To Get From One Life To Another Without Really Dying

How To Get From One Life To Another Without Really Dying

How to Survive the Ending of Your Life And Live To Create a New One

Sara Hart

Dawn City
Press

Copyright 2020 by Sara Hart

All rights reserved. Printed in the United States of America. No part of this book may be used or reproduced in any form or by any means, electronic or mechanical, without written permission from the Publisher except in the case of brief quotations embodied in critical articles and reviews.

For information: Dawn City Press
PO Box 711452
Oak Hill, VA 20171
email: info@dawncity.com

Library of Congress Control Number: 2020941559
ISBN: 978-0578705132

Contents

1. Our Multiple Lives 1

2. A Closer Look at the Between Lives Symptoms 17

3. The Inside Story of the Between Lives State 33

4. The Tomb and The Womb:
   Coping with Two Stages of the BLS 41

5. Survival Strategies:
   Helpful Hints for a Trek through the BLS 55

6. Enchantments: Getting Stuck in the BLS 63

7. Helping Teenagers Survive
   the BLS of Adolescence 75

8. Helping Someone through a Suicidal Crisis 89

9. Helping Yourself through a Suicidal Crisis
   When No Other Help is at Hand 107

10. How to Live Multiple Lives
    Without the Trauma of the BLS 115

11. Implications of My Research Findings 125

Preface

I am a prime example of someone who has lived several ego lives during this one lifetime, and can easily attest to the advantages — and the traumas — of staying on the planet through the Between Lives Process of life transitions. I can also attest to the dilemma of getting stuck between lives, as I have a somewhat "fixed" nature, and am slow to make necessary changes. I have also been a spiritual aspirant for all of my adult life, and like many such aspirants, I suffered for many years from dysfunctional idealism.

Additionally, I have always valued the work that the world does not value: the hands-on job of working with children. My own four children were so close in age that for seven years at least three of them were teenagers at the same time — and I have the scars to prove it! I then spent many years as counselor to approximately a thousand at-risk adolescents in residential treatment programs in three states, and taking that experience I designed and directed a program for behavior-disordered, abused adolescent girls. It became obvious to me that every teenager — no longer child and not yet adult — is in an extremely fragile between lives state, and in need of much support to get to the safety of a world-connected adult identity.

My interest in the subject of suicide began early, when I observed the suffering of a friend who experienced chronic severe depression and thought often of suicide. My brief encounter with such feelings of my own taught me that they are the most agonizing emotions that humans can endure. I began looking for answers to the issue of suicidal ideation while in graduate school;

and after earning my master's degree in rehab counseling I began my research in earnest by combing the literature at university campus libraries in three states to find what others had discovered on the subject. I was amazed to find that all the research had been done on the subject of suicidal crises, but none that I could find on the causes of suicidal ideation per se. If I wanted to find any answers, I would have to discover them myself.

I did my research by establishing a private counseling practice, developing a reputation as one who would deal with suicidal issues with compassion and respect, and over many years I worked with scores of people who were struggling with suicidal feelings. At some point I turned a corner in my understanding and discovered the amorphous phase of life where most suicidal feelings seemed to be occurring; I found they were connected to endings of world-connected life roles. Over time, I counted forty symptoms that my clients were vulnerable to while in this virtual Time Out from normal life. I dubbed it the Between Lives State (BLS) and it became the focus of my research. This book is the fruit of that research.

Sara Hart
North Myrtle Beach, South Carolina
July 2020

1

Our Multiple Lives

Today we are living out, in one lifetime, as many ego-lives as we have the strength and the courage to endure. Better health and nutrition standards have played a part in giving us an enormously extended life span, and unlimited opportunities abound for developing all of our potential. This phenomenon has always existed to some degree, I'm sure, but its occurrence has only recently reached epidemic proportions. In times past, most of us would not have had to worry about how to create a new life for ourselves after one lifetime ended. The physical life expectancy was only forty-eight years as recently as the year 1900. One hundred years later, it had risen to the upper seventies, and now in the year 2020, in many countries, life expectancy is well into the eighties. Those of us on the planet today are the first generations with the life expectancy of three quarters of a century, and the good health to enjoy it. We are the first generations with the whole world at our fingertips, and with so many options for living fully and richly, for developing every facet of our soul, every talent that we value ourselves for. We are the first generations ever given the incredible blessing of living through the ending of our lives — those seemingly unshakeable roles as parents, spouses, workers — and surviving to create entirely new ones.

The downside to this blessing is the necessity of surviving the disappearance of our familiar reality, a disappearance that marginalizes that facet of our self with which we had been identifying. In fact, surviving this disappearance requires us to contend with a process of "conscious reincarnation," wherein a void seems to engulf us, and this void tends to persist until our next life expression is born. Understanding this process is crucial to a trauma-free passage to our new life. This valley of shadows between lives need not be feared, for it is an integral part of this blessing in disguise. When we have lived out one role to its conclusion, we may regroup, retrain, revise our life script, and go forth once more, in an entirely new direction, creating a whole new life scenario that uses newly emerging facets of our self and expanding our consciousness beyond the realm of our most recently ended ego-lifetime.

Conscious reincarnation is not as far-fetched an idea as it at first may seem. Take our childhood, for example. Most of us remember it well. But we could also characterize that childhood as a "past life," since we are now so changed from who we were as a child. Looking back on that child, we see another person, not our current self. Yet our child self didn't have to physically die in order for our adult self to be born.

How many ego-identities might we expect to live out during one lifetime? If we are considering the identities that our ego may serially attach to and detach from as we are transformed from infancy to adulthood and beyond, in the course of a normal life span these identity changes might follow a typical pattern, such as: from child, through adolescence, to adulthood; from dependence to independence; from single to sharing a commitment; from carefree to parenthood; from married to single; from householder to worker in the world; from one career to another (we may commonly embrace as many as five, perhaps even more different career identities in one lifetime); from youthful to middle aged; from involved to sidelined; from healthy to infirm; from independent to dependent; and ultimately, to the last transition:

from physical life to the beyond. For most of us, our typical ego-lives could number at least ten. In addition to these normal transitions of a typical life, our world can be irrevocably changed by unexpected events over which we have no control. And today the world is changing so rapidly that we can, at any moment, find that the world as we knew it has disappeared, replaced by an unfamiliar reality.

Such endings and disruptions can catapult us into a "Between Lives State" (BLS) while we are still in a state of shock. But if we understand the nature of the BLS, we will be better prepared to deal with the surprise endings in life and the adjustment period that follows. I am here to cast a light on this phase of life between lives, and to point to a path through it that minimizes the negatives and emphasizes its many positives.

Perhaps the most important thing to know about the Between Lives State is that these periods between viable world-connected identities are always periods when we are vulnerable to at least forty BLS symptoms, ranging from disorientation to suicidal crises. We therefore need to be aware of the BLS hazards and take vigilant care of ourselves as we shed one outgrown ego-identity and develop a new, revised one to fit our new life experience. The purpose of this book is to shed light upon this amorphous stage of transition and give you the tools to glide through this valley of shadows as swiftly and painlessly as possible.

You will not have to travel alone. Many others are trekking through this valley — those whose lives have disappeared through natural or manmade disasters; those whose lives have ended through success, or failure, or simply through the natural flow of events that brought to a close a significant chapter of their lives. This book is for the empty-nester who has graduated from raising children, but can't get out of bed because she no longer knows who she is. It's for the clinically depressed retiree who feels lost without the purposeful identity he left at the office. It's for the widow and widower who lost their familiar lives when they lost their spouses. It's for all persons caught between jobs, between relationships, between lives. It's for those who've outgrown their life-connected identity but don't yet have a new one. It's for the upwardly mobile caterpillar who finds himself in the vulnerable chrysalis state without the benefit of a cocoon. It's for those who wouldn't mind going to sleep and never waking up again. It's for everyone who's ever felt suicidal and/or known someone who has. It is also written for all our friends and psychotherapists who must deal with us when we are struggling with the confusing issues of this Between Lives State.

Getting to Know the Valley of Shadows

When you experience a great loss in your life: the loss of a loved one, the loss of a way of life, the loss of what was your reality; when you have lost your worldly identity that was so recently valid in that vanished life; when your world has been shaken so violently that it will never again be the same, you experience what may feel like your own "death," even while you continue to live and breathe and appear to all around you to be unchanged. If you were a caterpillar, you would be weaving a cocoon right about now, for this is truly a most vulnerable stage of life, and you need a safe environment for your changing self while you go through it.

The Between Lives State phenomenon happens like this: As you go through life, your ego — your "I am" — becomes identified with, and attached to, the various roles that you play in the world. You may experience yourself as spouse, parent, employee, and other roles that connect you to your worldly life. When a significant world-connected role is no longer relevant to your life, that connection to your world ends. You cannot continue to live your role of spouse if your partner has left the stage. You mourn your partner's death, but you also experience your own "death" as the spouse that you were. Nor can you be the director of a department in a company that has "downsized" or retired you. And your reward for shepherding your children into adult lives of their own is that your identity as a hands-on parent is taken from you. If your lost role was a major ego-identity for you, its termination can have a significant impact upon your psyche, abruptly erasing your purpose for getting up every morning. This loss can confuse you into believing that your life is literally finished and that all you can do is mark time until you die, and that time feels imminent.

The greatest problem with getting through this amorphous phase of life between lives is that we have been unaware of its existence and, therefore, we've not known what to expect nor how to take care of ourselves while in this void. It has never been clearly identified before, much less understood for the "virtual death" experience that it is. This lack of understanding has caused us much unnecessary suffering. Even the professionals who endeavor to help us through life traumas have not been aware of the BLS and its side effects, thus having to find some other explanation for our obvious "thought disorders." The Between Lives State can be a time of great confusion, anxiety and sometimes even trauma and crisis. A detached ego, like a detached retina, gives us a grossly distorted view of things.

The good news is that, once we understand this strange territory between lives and learn how to travel through it with awareness and care, most of these symptoms can be lightened considerably, and the worst symptoms can be avoided entirely. At its worst, the BLS can transform minor frustrating circumstances into dangerous suicidal crises. At its best, it can be a lighthearted, temporary vacation from life with the opportunity to consciously design our future life expression. Furthermore, when we are aware of the BLS phenomenon, time spent there is considerably shortened, lasting approximately four to six months, compared to the twelve to thirty-six months for those who haven't a clue.

Exploring a Mystery

I began my research forty years ago to find out the mysterious dynamics at the heart of suicidal feelings, never suspecting that I would find the BLS. I did this research strictly to answer my own questions after witnessing the severe suffering of someone close to me as she struggled with chronic suicidal feelings, and the world's bizarre reactions to her pain. I had experienced suicidal feelings myself, and I could see that the world's perceptions of suicidal issues were very mistaken, making the typical response terribly misguided, dangerously off the mark, and always addressing that possible future event rather than the suffering of the present moment. The disparity between what I knew my friend was suffering and the weird, sometimes even hostile reactions of others to her pain stirred my curiosity deeply, and I vowed to discover the truth about suicidal issues.

During my exploration of suicidal issues through my private counseling practice, I stumbled across the BLS, and discovered that this was where most suicidal "ideation" seemed to be occurring. Over time, I identified at least forty symptoms and side effects that we're vulnerable to while in the BLS. Not knowing about this between lives phenomenon, we've tended to view these symptoms as evidence that something is drastically wrong with us, and they bring up every self-doubt we've ever had. If we become preoccupied with our symptoms, we complicate our trip through the maze that can lead us to a new life. A serious pressure factor in the Between Lives State is that the world does not recognize our fragile condition. It still expects "normal" behavior from us; it makes demands that we're likely to feel unable to meet in a normal fashion. These demands often force us to continue moving through a routine that no longer seems to have meaning for us.

Ultimately, the way to end our vulnerability to these symptoms is simply to reestablish a connection to the world with another facet of our self — a revised ego-identity — in a role for which we value ourselves, for it is this self-value that is the necessary key to feeling alive. Until then, we will be vulnerable to the BLS symptoms, and therefore, we should know what to expect and how to cope with them. There are hundreds of books out there that tell us how to create a new life. But I've not found one that exposes this enervating phase of life between lives, nor advises us how to get safely through it.

Suicidal Feelings a BLS Phenomenon?

After I made this mysterious phase of life the focus of my research, I noticed that people with firmly connected ego-identities often endured incredible hardships, crushing traumas, and devastating losses without ever having a suicidal thought, while those whose ego-identities had disappeared could be thrown into a suicidal crisis, literally, by a bad hair day. These disparate reactions occurred consistently among the people with whom I worked. Without exception, every suicidal person who learned about the Between Lives State identified with my description of it. A few claimed to be experiencing all forty symptoms at once. Some harbored a fear that they were seriously mentally ill.

Between Lives people appreciated the dark humor of my tentative "diagnosis." I would reassure them, "The good news is, you're probably not mentally ill. The bad news is, you may be 'dead!'" While such a statement might horrify a person firmly connected to life, it so accurately described what the between lives people were experiencing, they invariably grinned broadly with appreciation. To finally have their condition defined and understood meant that there may be a remedy in sight. As I worked with them, they came to see their condition as an uncomfortable but temporary phase of life that could be moved through more swiftly with their enlightened cooperation. All expressed relief at having a label to impose upon their condition, reducing the problem to a manageable size and taking it out of the realm of hopeless melodrama. Of course, a few of them asked if it wouldn't be easier just to leave their body, if indeed they were as dead as they felt. It was at this point that I would present some of the practical advantages of keeping their current body for use in their next life.

Advantages of Living through this Transition

Imagine being a full-grown adult at birth, with a high school diploma and perhaps even a college degree already in your pocket. I remind my suicidal clients that there are some real and significant perks attached to their current body. If they stay in them while they endure the experience of their ego-death and eventual rebirth, they will be able to enter their next life as the adult they are, bringing with them all their degrees and credentials, as well as the wisdom and experience they've gained from all the valuable lessons they've learned the hard way in their most recent past life. They'll have all the good karma from their "past life" but they will not have to start over as a weak and clueless babe, nor break in two new parents. They will not have to go through potty training, nor attend school all over again, nor face any of the traumas that those who believe in reincarnation envision.

Another significant advantage: If they stay in their current body, they can participate consciously in the process of creating their next life, choosing to go in a new direction and do the things that give them joy, using the talents for which they value themselves most. These are very big advantages that are attached to their psyche through their connection to their current body, and are transferable to their next life only if it takes place in this same body.

If, however, they choose to abandon their body and leave the planet at this point, I don't know what happens and therefore can hold out no guarantees. I've heard that heaven is a gated community and that getting in without a reservation could be a problem.

Hamlet spoke about the dilemma of not knowing for sure what comes after suicide in his soliloquy. "But in that sleep of death," he wondered aloud, "what dreams may come . . ." Could it be a case of jumping out of the frying pan and into the fire? Have we attempted unsuccessfully to solve our problems through suicide in past lives? Is there such a thing as past lives? Or future lives? We just don't know. As Hamlet concluded, ". . . must give us pause."

But one thing I do know for sure: Any credentials and degrees earned this lifetime will remain in the pocket of the current body, wherever our spirit goes. Surely everyone would agree that this would be a dreadful waste!

Nobody Likes the BLS

By the time we are adults, we have experienced the symptoms of the chrysalis state more than we cared to, for the process of psychological maturation that ends our childhood and adolescence is a long series of natural ego-deaths and rebirths. It is the BLS phenomenon that makes adolescence so volatile and weird, and teenagers so unstable and unpredictable. We didn't enjoy the symptoms brought on by the constant flux and change of our fragile ego-identity during our adolescence, and would not willingly volunteer to enter into the process again.

Spending our Life in a Tomb

One of our most effective survival skills, developed, no doubt, during our Neanderthal days, is the ingenious technique of avoidance. In our dread of entering the Between Lives State, we sometimes avoid taking the risks involved with releasing that which is ending to create a new life, choosing instead to cling to a deadening or abusive relationship, a deadly boring job, or some other lifeless state — which ironically can become the very psychological tomb we had wished to avoid.

But when we attempt to peer into an unknown future, we see only a foggy, barren landscape that threatens to drop off into an abyss. If there is such a thing as a "future," we suspect that it would lie on the other side of that abyss. Just thinking of it tends to bring up all our insecurities and send us skittering back to our safe but boring tomb, where we choose to keep trudging through our daily routines like sleepwalkers, chronically depressed. When chronic fatigue has no physical cause, it may well be a phenomenon of the Between Lives State, our heart's reaction to our remaining in a tomb-like life.

Vacating our Lives Temporarily

One common way we experience the Between Lives State all the time is the annual tradition we call vacation. We vacate our "real" lives and make a holiday of it. The whole point of a vacation is to do something not ordinary to our daily routine, to get in touch with the fun of life, to recreate our zest for life — the true meaning of recreation. We step out of our ordinary life and try to experience ourselves and the world from a carefree point of view. Carefree because we temporarily break the connection to our "real" life where our cares remain.

Vacations can be a great Time Out period to take stock of our lives: where we've been so far, and where we want to go in the future. We have the leisure and the objectivity while on vacation to look at our life and decide if we want to take a different direction once we enter Time again. Getting perspective about our life is also one of the advantages of being between lives, provided we can learn to recognize and manage the sometimes uncomfortable side effects and symptoms that go with it.

Precipitating Factors of the BLS

Some examples of ego-life-ending events that could set off our experience of the BLS symptoms are: the death of or divorce from a spouse, an event that ends our own ego-identity as spouse; the publishing of the book or the ending of any major project we've been identifying with for some time; the end of our role as active parent (the "empty nest" syndrome); a retirement, downsizing, or promotion that dramatically alters who we perceive our self to be in the work world; a permanent dislocation as a result of war or natural disaster; a relocation because of a career move; a major disillusionment that destroys our beliefs about life, our world and/or our place in it, our beliefs about other people or our self; a disabling disease or accident, or simply the natural progression of the aging process that makes us aware that we cannot be in the world the person we have perceived our self to be, or expected that we would become (the "mid-life crisis"). Such ego-ending scenarios are as varied and numerous as are we humans.

Forty Symptoms of the Between Lives State

The symptoms/side effects that we typically experience in the BLS tend to begin more or less immediately after one of those events in our life that brings to an end the ego-identity that we had up to that point been living out. Sometimes their onset is gradual; sometimes instantaneous. The first three symptoms typically manifest at once. The others appear in no particular order that I have been able to discern. And while some stem from the same source — a disconnect from feelings, for example — the manifestations can be different, such as loss of libido or emotional numbness, among others. (If reading this list becomes too overwhelming, just skip ahead, and refer back to it as needed.)

1. *Shock* - Mental and emotional paralysis.
2. *Disorientation* - Confusion about what's happened, what to think, feel or do.
3. *Loss of ego-identity* - Disconnection from one's vital, world-connected life role.
4. *Lack of energy* - Disconnection from the energy source that one's life role provided.
5. *Sleep disorders* - Insomnia, chronic need to sleep, troubled dreams, frequent awakening during night.
6. *Confusion about life's purpose* - Disrupted belief system.
7. *Loss of perspective* - Disrupted belief system.
8. *Loss of interest in everything* - Disconnection from the world.
9. *Loss of sense of humor* - Loss of perspective.
10. *Loss of libido* - Disconnection from feelings.
11. *Loss of sense of joy* - Disconnection from feelings.
12. *Emotional numbness* - Disconnection from feelings.
13. *Loss of confidence* - In self, in life, in one's ability to cope.
14. *Loss of social poise* - Loss of ego-centeredness.
15. *Feelings of isolation* - Inability to communicate one's confusing condition to others.
16. *Loss of self-esteem* - One's sense of self-worth disappears along with one's lost ego-identity.

17. *Inability to carry on conversation* - Basis for opinions is lost when that basis was tied to one's role in life.
18. *Chronic anxiety* - Caused by the mind's ceaseless attempts to adjust to the unknown.
19. *Reclusiveness* - Dread of social contact due to a profound sense of vulnerability.
20. *Chronic low-grade depression* - Chronic sense of loss of connection to life.
21. *Loss of hope* - Lost reality destroys the basis for hope.
22. *Loss of trust of Life* - If reality can disappear, nothing can be trusted.
23. *Loss of faith in God* - Disrupted belief system.
24. *Nausea of life* - A mix of despair, disgust, anger, grief.
25. *Feeling that life has no meaning* - Loss of meaning of one's own life.
26. *Profound disillusionment* - Loss of belief that all life — not just one's own — has meaning.
27. *Feelings of powerlessness* - Disrupted belief system.
28. *Nervous breakdown episodes* - Disrupted coping system.
29. *Anger* - Resistant response to the loss of power to control one's life.
30. *Rage* - Aggressive reaction to powerlessness to control one's life.

31. *Despair* - Hopelessness, grief upon acceptance of powerlessness over aversive circumstances.
32. *Profound depression* – Arising from the heart's experience of its virtual death, an enchanted state, whereby one is temporarily blind to any other way of being.
33. *Carelessness with one's physical appearance* - Disconnection from life.
34. *Carelessness with one's physical well-being* - Disconnection from life.
35. *Slow suicide through neglect, apathy* - Disconnection from life.
36. *Suicidal feelings when pressured by minor life crises* - Presented by the mind as a valid solution.
37. *Suicidal feelings when symptoms become overwhelming* - Presented by the mind as a way to escape severe pressure.
38. *Suicidal crisis when overwhelmed by aversive worldly demands* - Belief that it's the only possible solution to unavoidable and serious problems. The most extreme coping of the powerless — it is an enchanted state.
39. *Alienation* - Feeling that one no longer "belongs" anywhere in society/the world.
40. *Suicide attempt* - Attempt to drop the overwhelming burden that life has become.

Getting a Grip on Perspective

Experiencing several of these symptoms at once suggests the possibility that you are currently between lives, and therefore may be vulnerable to any or all the other symptoms as well. It is important to remember that this weird state of being is actually a normal part of the process of psychological transformation, and a temporary phase of the extended lives we are leading today. As Soul, you have not died. The life that has ceased to exist was merely one facet of your soul-expression.

It also helps to keep in mind that you can minimize the impact of these temporary symptoms, once you understand them to be merely side effects of this rather bizarre stage of life where Nature forgot to provide you with a protective cocoon while stripping you of a socially acceptable ego-identity.

2

A Closer Look at the Between Lives Symptoms

Most of the symptoms encountered in the Between Lives State are not unfamiliar to us. They are composed of the very human thoughts and feelings that we experience off and on at various times throughout our lives. They are not usually severely disturbing to us when they're experienced one at a time and while we possess a world-connected ego-identity to help us keep a sane perspective and deal effectively with them. It is only when we are between lives that so many of these symptoms assail us at once. And because we have no ego-identity "plugged into" life at that time, we can easily become confused and overwhelmed, creating the distressing trauma of the Between Lives State. Let's look more closely at some of the symptoms mentioned in the previous chapter.

Shock

When we find that we have been kicked out of our life as we knew it — through the death of a spouse, the ending of a career, even the successful completion of an all-absorbing major project — we can find ourselves in a state of shock. Our thoughts and feelings are thrown off their familiar track, and we don't know what to think or feel at this point. We see the outer fact of that which has ended, but since we don't perceive what has happened to our ego-identity, we don't understand why we are so psychologically stunned.

Disorientation

Most of the habits that had kept us on track in our recent ego-life now seem irrelevant to this limbo state, and we suddenly find ourselves without a life-pattern that would allow us to take our next step for granted. Nothing in that lifetime had prepared us for this crisis.

Meanwhile, the world exhorts us to just keep on moving! But in order to do so we must know where to place our foot for the next step, and in our disoriented condition that next step is not at all clear. If you've ever felt lost in a crowded airport terminal, you know how distressing it is to be jostled about by the hurrying travelers who have some sense of where they're going. You feel the need to get on the sidelines of the hurrying world until you gain some sense of direction. Staying still feels like the only activity that fits the circumstances, and may be the wisest course to take.

"After my last child's departure," reported a woman in one of my Life Transitions support groups, speaking about her Empty Nest period, "I just sat for the next three months, with no idea what else to do but sit."

Chronic need to sleep

Speaking of that period right after graduation from college, a young man in the group said, "Some days, sleeping was the only thing I wanted to do. I couldn't seem to stay awake."

Sleep is probably the most benign "survival behavior" we have while coping with this Between Lives phenomenon. Survival behaviors are those gut-level skills that helped us continue as a species when we were otherwise powerless in aversive circumstances. They're the skills we used during our powerless childhood, and they're the skills we fall back on whenever, as adults, we feel powerless. They are actually the primitive adaptive powers of the powerless. I'm sure there were times when being overtaken by sleep in the safety of a cave was the only thing that enabled us humans to survive. This power to endure has served us well through the ages, giving these survival behaviors a very strong hold on our psyche. These behaviors can and do emerge full blown whenever we find ourselves in a life circumstance where our more sophisticated, learned behaviors have proven insufficient in dealing effectively with an unanticipated crisis, and we feel utterly powerless. Sleep can be healing. But, like all the primitive survival behaviors, it becomes problematic when it interferes with normal living.

Insomnia

Ironically, as much as we may feel the need to sleep when we should be awake, we may find ourselves awakening in the middle of the night, unable to go back to sleep even though we're exhausted. Insomnia, another Between Lives symptom, seems linked to subliminal anxiety, which can be chronic in the Between Lives State. Anxiety is usually the culprit that's involved in this symptom.

Chronic low-grade anxiety

We humans have survived as a species because of our natural tendency to adapt, to adjust to circumstances. But we need facts in order to adjust to them. When the structure of our life has been taken away and we don't as yet see a new structure, nor information that could facilitate that adjustment — as is often the case when in the BLS — a constant state of anxiety may develop. Its cause is the mind's ongoing vigilance in attempting to adjust to . . . it knows not what. The mind's problem-solving efforts become circular, with our thoughts always returning to, and being disrupted by the void created by the missing information, preventing an effective adjustment that would quiet the mind. This process can be so unsettling that it disturbs our sleep. It is this frustrated adjustment energy that manifests as anxiety.

Lack of energy

Our lack of energy baffles us, because we don't realize how crucial a role our imagination plays in the flow of energy to function in the world, nor how vital to our daily motivation is our perceived identity in the world. The real significance is that my mental image of myself as this particular person in the world creates a "closed circuit," much like an electrical circuit, within my imagination. This imaginative circuit connects my psyche to the world, a circuit through which my energy flows to serve my perceived worldly role. And when that role ends, my connection to the world and to that life is interrupted, and the energy circuit is broken. Like an unplugged electrical appliance, I will experience no energy flow. Faith has occasionally been has aptly compared to electricity, and that analogy seems to apply here: when I no longer have this inner "knowing" of who I am in the world, this is a crucial disruption of "faith" within my consciousness, which causes the "break" in my connection to life and the cessation of energy flow between my psyche and the world. This absence of energy is a major symptom of the Between Lives State.

Loss of life's purpose and meaning

The thing that gets us up and out of bed in the morning is our connection to "purpose" in our lives. We don't ordinarily question every day why we have to get moving. The normal pressures of daily living make us turn off the alarm and reach for that cup of caffeine to give us the energy we need to face the daily grind. But it's not the daily grind that gets us up. It's that subliminal connection to our life behind it all that makes us take it for granted that we will enter the day. This connection undergirds our reason for living and gives meaning and purpose to our being.

When life as we know it ends, that connection to purpose goes with it, taking away the meaning of our life and leaving us floundering in an internal confusion. We may still have to get moving, but we can't remember why, exactly. The most routine things toward which we move have lost their value, since they were vitally connected to our past sense of purpose. And as the ongoing worldly duties seem to have no intrinsic value to us now, we experience these remaining obligations as burdensome. The complete absence of energy makes them seem impossible to accomplish. Besides, we just don't have the heart for doing them.

Be grateful for habits. Habit may be enough to keep us moving our bodies through the routine day, at least until we develop a new meaning and purpose that will reconnect our being to life and refuel our motivation.

Unless we have a strategy for getting ourselves out of bed without daily soul-searching for a good reason to get up, we could experience a mini-suicidal crisis every morning of our journey between lives, finding ourselves sitting on the edge of our bed reciting Hamlet's soliloquy: "To be ... or not to be... that is the question." ... Obviously an unwelcome emotional drain.

The best strategy here is to make a rule for ourselves that we are not allowed to "question" life in general and our life in particular first thing in the morning during the process of getting up. Our best friends at this time are our old habit patterns that move us through a habitual morning ritual without the need for thought: get that cup of coffee or tea, read the newspaper, watch the morning wakeup show, do some yoga. Our mind does not need to entertain thoughts about anything other than the steps we're taking out of habit. It's also helpful to have a daily inspirational reading to attend to each morning that keeps us connected to our cosmic reasons for being on Earth. It's a great lifeline during the Between Lives period. While in this state, we need to know that it is cosmically enough to get up every day for the simple purpose of nurturing the only soul that God has made us steward of for this entire lifetime — our own self.

Loss of perspective when pressured by minor life crises

A very confusing factor in having our "life" end is that to a casual observer not much seems to have really changed for us. Yet from our perspective, nothing is the same. A young seeker after truth climbed to the top of a snow covered mountain to ask a wise old man sitting there, "What is Life?" The wise man looked out over the mountain range for a long moment, and then said with a sigh, "Life is just one darned thing after another!"

At times this seems to be an accurate definition of life. And some days we handle life's aggravations better than others. But if a water pipe should burst on the same day that our phone goes out of order, and the car won't start, we wouldn't be surprised if we eventually developed a tension headache as a result of this frustrating set of circumstances.

However, a person in the Between Lives State, given the same circumstances, might react with more than a tension headache. He could be thrown into a serious suicidal crisis. Such a person is already stressed to the max by the Between Lives symptoms. And when he's confronted by even minor life crises, the combination of symptoms tends to prevent a sane perspective, rational thinking, or effective action. This can allow the seriousness of the situation to become blown dangerously out of proportion. This inability to cope with everyday crises and the frustration thus generated can precipitate an active suicidal crisis in no time flat. To a Between Lives person, sometimes suicide can compute as the only solution possible. Because of this lack of perspective and the relatively distorted thinking of a person who has lost his world-connected ego-identity, it's easy to become completely overwhelmed in this state.

For this reason, it is vitally important, while in the BLS, that we never neglect the little daily-life tasks until too many things slide into disrepair, especially since such neglect is a common human inclination in the best of times. But when we're in this no-energy, unmotivated, ego-disintegrated state, that's precisely what we're likely to do. We just let things slide. The appointed day for getting the oil changed in our car comes and goes without action. The broken fridge door must be slammed ever harder each day, but we ignore it. The kitchen faucet seems loose where it should be tight. The front door resists being opened. The back door, swollen from rain, is hard to close. Sooner or later, they all give up at the same time: the car breaks down, the refrigerator door finally falls off, the leaky faucet suddenly becomes a geyser, the front door won't open, the back door won't close! Such a state of affairs would overwhelm even an enthusiastic person fully invested in life with all his energy at his disposal. For a Between Lives person such a time becomes a life-threatening crisis which, at the very least, subjects him to miserable feelings of despair and a further draining of his precious little remaining energy. But at the worst, the crisis leads to suicide as the most tragic of survival coping behaviors.

When such a crisis happens to us, we need to immediately get in touch with a therapeutic person who can facilitate the re-establishment of perspective, help us sort out priorities and make a realistic plan for getting everything back in working order. Why attempt this alone when a friend or professional can provide an instant support group and can help us regain a balanced perspective?

Loss of interest in everything

"I had always looked forward to taking up painting again after my kids were grown," an empty nester told me. "But now that they're gone and I have all the time in the world, painting has no appeal for me, nor do any of the other hobbies that I used to enjoy."

Few things are more depressing than to turn to those activities that used to give us pleasure and comfort only to find that they've lost all meaning for us. But that's a typical — and temporary — reaction when between lives. It's a good idea to keep inviting ourselves gently to such activities, because sooner or later the interest will return along with the enthusiasm we used to experience. And new interests will emerge, as well.

Dullness of mind

Not only can our hobbies lose their appeal, but interest in everything can disappear. Newspapers and the evening news, once important to us, seem so irrelevant now. Even something as simple as sending a birthday card to a friend can seem like a meaningless chore. It's hard to believe that people "out there" are still having birthdays anyway, while Time has seemingly ended for us. In this frame of mind, we have nothing to say to anyone, and we may not be interested in anything anyone else says either, because we've lost the context in which to receive and process information. The intellect tends to shut down and we experience a pervasive dullness of mind. It's amazing how the loss of our identity-in-the-world reverberates throughout every facet of our lives.

Loss of sense of humor

The Between Lives symptoms would be easier to handle with the help of our sense of humor. We might agree with the comedian mangled in an auto accident when he reported to rescuers, "It only hurts when I laugh." Unfortunately, the loss of our sense of humor is another of the temporary casualties of being suspended between lives. It's very scary for those of us who rely on humor for taking life lightly. It's also a pity to lose our appreciation for the absurd just now, because the Between Lives State is filled with many absurdities. While the loss is temporary, the heart — the mother of all feelings, who dwells in the eternal Now — is experiencing the loss as eternal.

Emotional paralysis

There is a temporary paralysis that sets in, numbing our emotions. We just don't feel anything. Nothing moves us, often not even fear. If we're already "dead," what further harm can possibly be inflicted upon us? This, of course, is a subconscious reaction, but then that's where fear reactions come from, too. Sympathy for others can disappear, as well. It's difficult to sympathize with someone who's sick when we're experiencing ourselves as not even living. This emotional paralysis can make us feel less than human, one more reason it's important to remember that it is just another temporary phenomenon of the Between Lives State, one more BLS "joke" that we are in no mood to appreciate at the moment.

Another facet of this emotional paralysis manifests as loss of libido and its close cousin: joy. They seem so very dead that it isn't even conceivable by our minds that they will ever return. Never fear, they will reappear as new life begins to stir within — as it eventually will.

Chronic low-grade depression

Depression may be another of those misunderstood survival skills — a primitive mode of comforting our most primal self, when we feel powerless in an aversive circumstance. If, instead of running from our depression, we embrace it as an attempt at internal comforting, we may find our depression turning into a comforting bliss.

Depression, in general, is connected to the adjustment process of our mind and heart — our heart mourning the loss of something that's left our lives, and the extinction within our mind of some long-cherished expectation. A grieving mother, who had lost her nine-year-old son in an auto accident, told me of an unexpected facet of her grief process. "As I watched my son grow each year, I had dreamed of one day holding his children in my arms. Now that he's gone, I'm having to face the fact that this will never happen." Not only was she grieving for the loss of her son in her life, she was giving up her expectation of her future grandchildren. She was mourning for what could never be.

Chronic low-grade depression is a normal condition of the Between Lives State. It seems that our body chemistry tends to change to correspond with the condition the psyche is experiencing — its disconnection from life. Even the metabolism seems to slow down, as if the body has gone into hibernation, which can make us feel reluctant to move about more than absolutely necessary.

Profound depression

This symptom of the BLS, a deeper experience of depression, brings with it a more radical change of body chemistry. When in this condition, we tend to be experiencing our own ego death-state profoundly. The imagination ceases to function as a problem-solving mechanism, no longer looking for other life options. It is akin to an enchantment, a temporary condition where we are blind to any other way to perceive our current "reality." For these reasons it is experienced by us as hopelessness. This was the case with an elderly widower, whose concerned daughter came to me for advice on how to help her father after his wife died. In this state he could not help himself, nor did it occur to him to do so. This made his prognosis a negative one.

There is hope for the hopeless. Fortunately, there are effective new medications that work well to restore the body chemistry to its natural balance. However, it's fairly obvious that we also need to be working on breaking the psychological enchantment of being "dead to the world," and moving on through the Between

Lives process toward life again, if we are to successfully pull out of this living-death experience.

The swiftest and easiest way to do that is through a therapist-led support group for people between lives. Sometimes a person in this state needs a friend or family member to gently push for seeking help, even taking him by the hand and leading him there. He may be unable to take the necessary steps on his own.

Loss of self-esteem, confidence, and social poise

Since our self-esteem and self-confidence are based on our comfort with who we are, it's no wonder that they suffer a setback when we're between lives — we are there precisely because we've lost our identity. It's very difficult to remain poised in social settings, since what we bring to such a setting is our self. Too bad we can't just hang a "Closed for Psychic Renovations" sign on our ego while we're undergoing these transitional changes. God knows, everyone should sympathize, because they also have Between Lives experiences periodically throughout their lives. Perhaps eventually, when we all understand the true nature of this chrysalis stage of life-transitions, we will have a way to signal our condition, and society will have an unspoken agreement to handle with care those of us who are undergoing one of our periodic ego-identity transformations. Perhaps there will also be Life Transitions support groups in every community that we can visit when we realize we're in the Between Lives State again. Hanging out with other people who are between lives makes us feel normal again, and we find ourselves laughing as we compare our Between Lives experiences. Support groups are the quickest way to regain our perspective in the BLS.

Feelings of isolation

An elderly woman's adjustment to widowhood was made much more painful by the inability of her "couples" friends to be supportive of her during the time of transition from wife to widow.

While in the Between Lives State, our inability to understand and verbalize our confusing feelings, and everyone else's inability to empathize, causes us to feel a poignant isolation, even when surrounded by friends and family.

Isolation is one of the most problematic symptoms, because it is usually one of the givens, along with a combination of other symptoms, in the precipitation of any suicidal crisis. Isolation is also one of the most painful symptoms of the Between Lives State, one that drives a suicidal person to desperately seek relief through some sort of contact. And when attempts to make healing contact fail, that failure can drive the seeker to attempt suicide.

"Nervous breakdown" episodes

A working definition of "nervous breakdown" is what happens when our old behavior that used to work well for us in our old reality no longer works; and, in our state of shock at this abrupt change, we keep looking back, not understanding that there is a new reality confronting us, demanding that we exhibit new behavior. This predicament leaves us stranded, open-mouthed, as our inner computer experiences a temporary "meltdown." It's another form of enchantment, wherein we become fixated with a mental and emotional paralysis when confronted by the disappearance of our perceived reality.

Anger

Anger may be a recurring feeling for those who have lost their life and their ego-identity through some life-changing event. Anger, in general, is a primitive inborn aggressive reaction to the perception of powerlessness to take care of ourselves, to be true to ourselves, to protect our ego-identity in an aversive situation. Anger asserts, "I am being made powerless here, and I won't stand for it!" Before we became reasonable, thinking creatures, anger may have been our only strength in dealing with many crises.

It galvanizes all of our energies in defense of our survival. But like all survival behaviors, while it "solves" problems, anger often creates additional problems for us, especially in the more complex world in which we live today.

We can solve our problem of powerlessness in any situation, and our anger will instantly dissolve, by first, wisely accepting the realistic fact that only God is Omnipotent. Since we are mere mortals, there will be limits to our power range. But within that limit, we still can find our legitimate power. We must search for and discover where our legitimate power can be found in the situation that evoked our anger reaction. In this paradigm, after we discover where we do have control, anger can be dissolved simply by "backing up" to the boundary where our power actually is.

For example, I cannot control the offensive, judgmental words coming out of someone else's mouth, but I can choose — and therefore control — what I'm willing to listen to. I can say to myself, "Fortunately, this person is not my judge!" taking away any power I may have inadvertently assigned to him that had caused me to feel vulnerable to his negative opinion for an angry moment. Then I can honor his need to be foolishly judgmental in his own universe, but refuse to allow him any power in mine, nor give him the power of my attention.

When I remember this strategy, my anger will instantly dissolve by the reclaiming of my personal power. And the desire to punch the person spouting the offending words also dissipates instantly, for I have reclaimed my power to take care of myself in that situation without causing myself more problems — an apt definition of mature behavior.

Anger stimulated by the loss of our ego-identity must be handled in a similar fashion. We cannot undo the death of our spouse nor a dismissal from our life's work. We have no power to undo these events that have taken our ego-identity from us.

Both circumstances can evoke anger. It can seem impossible to reclaim our power here.

In such cases we must resort to "cosmic" thinking. Yes, our life as we knew it has been taken away by that defining event. But in the cosmic scheme of things, we are more than spouse or employee. We are each a unique expression of the universe, equally as important to the makeup of the cosmos as every other soul. As a still living, breathing soul, it becomes our task, when between lives, to discover what next "assignment" we will choose, what new part we will play on the universal stage of life. We must now seek out a new way of being ourself on Earth in a new life role. The saying that "when one door closes, another door opens" applies here. Our anger reaction beats in frustration on the door that has closed. Our wisdom reaction accepts our lack of power over the closed door, and turns our attention toward looking for the door that is opening to a new life expression.

Rage

Rage may be a rare reaction to the end of one's ego-life, but in some at-risk people, it can precipitate an acute homicidal/suicidal crisis. Rage is an aggressive reaction to the perception of powerlessness by those with an extreme need for control over everything in their lives. This aggressive reaction is more likely to occur in a person who has minimal healthy coping skills and who exhibits no tolerance for situations where he perceives himself to be powerless. An extreme example is found in one who returns to the workplace from which he was fired and kills those who still work there.

Alienation

The level of isolation from society represented by alienation limits our ability to receive help from what should be our potential support system. When our own confusing Between Lives State is so misunderstood by our world that we find our condition being misjudged and condemned as evidence of character defects within us, we have no words with which to defend ourselves or our condition. Nor do we have the heart for the endeavor, for their seemingly cold-hearted misunderstanding and misjudgments compound our sense of alienation, making reconnection seem out of the question. How can we turn to those who so misunderstand our dilemma that they discount any expression on our part of the situation as we see it. This drives us deeper into isolation. And the alienation is complete when we cease to see any world that we would want to return to.

Suicide Attempts

A suicidal crisis is usually caused by a sudden, unavoidable, worldly demand that overwhelms one's coping system, making suicide seem the only solution. Such an enchanted state of mind precludes any healthy perspective that could save one from making this fatal mistake.

Understanding is the Key

It is easy to see why an understanding of the Between Lives phenomenon with all its symptoms is so important. Such problematic feelings during a time that is also very confusing could lead, at the very least, to our making poor decisions, and at the most, to needless tragedy. While each symptom is a fairly normal, everyday feeling that we could experience at other times of our lives, when experienced together, they create this uncomfortable syndrome found only in the chrysalis phase of life, where we have been stripped of our former connection to life, and are forced to undergo the raw scrambled eggs process of transformation without the benefit of a protective cocoon.

Understanding this can help us to more quickly recognize the nature of this psychological state that we find ourselves in and the necessity to take care of ourselves with more conscious attention than usual. Consciously attending to the Between Lives process can make our passage through it more safe, swift, and sure.

All the symptoms — from disorientation to suicidal feelings — stimulated by the Between Lives State can be effectively dealt with and minimized once we realize they are just symptoms. We don't have to "believe" these symptoms, nor fall into an enchantment of the melodrama suggested by them, but we can simply reassure ourselves that, despite the symptoms, the world has not yet ended — evidenced by our still walking around in our familiar physical vehicle. We can let the symptoms merely alert us to our Between Lives status and of our need to take special care of ourselves at this time, seeking safety and support. Meanwhile, we can begin moving toward creating a new life for ourselves — always helpful in alleviating unwelcome Between Lives symptoms.

Equally important to remember is that our reward for staying on the planet and in our body through this symptom-filled transition is great: We will enter a new life as a new creature, but we will do so consciously, with all the advantages of being an adult from day one, with all the wisdom that life has taught us thus far, and with our hard-earned credentials, knowledge, and experiences tucked safely in our pocket. And when we're in the BLS, we are actually in a process that will automatically tend to flow toward a new life expression — if we don't become so enchanted with the melodramatic symptoms of the BLS that we forget to look for that door that is opening to new life.

3

The Inside Story of the BLS

I have come to envy the care that Mother Nature gives to the lowly caterpillar in her trek through the BLS. When she enters her cocoon, she leaves behind her ego-identity of caterpillar and surrenders herself to the mysterious process of metamorphosis that changes her into a different creature entirely. The problems associated with her loss of identity are no doubt minimized by nature's foresight in furnishing her with a cocoon for a sanctuary, safe from worldly demands and pressures while she undergoes a profound identity transformation. When she emerges as a butterfly, she probably has no memory of ever having been a caterpillar. Nor does she likely have traumatic flashbacks of being disassembled and becoming something similar to raw scrambled eggs before being put back together in a new way — as a beautiful winged creature.

We humans, on the other hand, blessed with infinitely more consciousness than either caterpillar or butterfly, must contend with the chrysalis phase of life fully conscious and with no nature-made sanctuary to protect us from the pressures of worldly demands while we undergo the raw scrambled eggs metamorphosis of our ego-identity. The challenge becomes: how to endure through the trials of identity transformation after the disappearance of our outgrown ego-identity and before we develop a new identity and a new way to be on Earth. Why so many symptoms, and why these symptoms? We have to look into our psyche to find the answers, for it's the thinking processes of our mind and heart reacting to our loss of "self in the world" that cause all of these uncomfortable symptoms.

To understand the inner, psychological dynamics brought on by the Between Lives State, we need to observe the two major aspects of our consciousness and their way of relating to each other. Using myself as a case study, let's for a moment assume the ending of my life as I know it through some outer event impacting my identity, such as my career as therapist ending. Any such life-changing event can take with it my identity of myself to the extent I experience "me" as intrinsically connected to that life role.

As a dual-faceted being with two minds, I will tend to experience two very different interpretations of the same event in two very different ways. My logical intellectual mind, always performing his role of interpreter of the outer facts of my life, will survey the outer scene and report to himself, "My therapy career has ended in the world. I don't see myself having a role out there any longer."

My intuitive heart has a mind of her own and her mode of thinking is experiential. She experiences my existence. And when I'm between lives, she experiences my non-existence. While my mind's mode of thinking is linear and logical, my intuitive heart has no desire to be logical. That is not her function. She does her thinking in images and feelings. Her function is to experience, to know, to be. And as the feminine aspect of my consciousness, she nurtures the seeds of creativity.

When my ego-identity becomes detached from its worldly connection, my heart will experience this as the absence of self-in-the-world. And since she lives in the eternal Now, it will feel to her like an "eternal" condition. At the moment, she's experiencing not being, as far as my identity in the world is concerned. And she cannot imagine a future existence because she cannot imagine a future, period. Whatever's happening now is happening eternally, as far as my heart is concerned.

Meanwhile of course, my mind, oblivious of my heart's needs and unaware of his cosmic responsibility to my heart, is looking out at the blank canvas upon which my heart's creation will in the future be expressed (ironically, by him) and is declaring matter-of-factly, "I can see there's nothing out there; and there's no point in pursuing nothing." This news causes my heart to sink.

Such status reports by my mind are taken at face value by my heart, and she tends to react unquestioningly to this as her inner "truth" in the eternal Now. She adjusts to her severance from life by automatically shutting down those parts of the psychic system that were relating to the world, breaking the psychological connections that allowed vital energies to flow into outer life and back again, so necessary to the feelings of being connected to life, so necessary to the sense of being alive, and so necessary to having energy!

It's the severing of these energy circuits that triggers the beginning of the syndrome of the detached ego-identity. It precipitates the onset of the forty other known symptoms/side effects — and heaven knows how many more as yet unidentified ones involved with this Between Lives State. These symptoms are merely the playing out of the tragi-comedy of miscommunications between my mind and my heart, as they try to cope with and adjust to what each is experiencing and perceiving, as a result of my career coming to an end and its attendant loss of my world-connected ego-identity.

Who's Minding the Consciousness?

If my two minds were on good terms, and if the logical mind were properly mature and wise, he would understand the heart's way of experiencing my current non-existence and he would be able to give her perspective, with feedback regarding the facts of both the inner and the outer worlds: "We as a soul are still here," he would reassure her. "It's just that our identity as therapist in the world has ended 'out there,' and we don't yet know how we will identify ourselves in the world in the time to come." One of his mature functions is to maintain a realistic and healthy perspective, facilitating the heart's appropriate inner adjustments to outer conditions.

As it is, given the uneven development of my mind and heart, both aspects of my consciousness are very likely to become temporarily thrown off their individual tracks by my loss of ego-identity. And the conversations between the two in these circumstances can be downright ludicrous. Because the intuitive heart is mute — her "voice" is expressed through imagery, feeling, and intuitive knowing — and because the relationship between the mind and heart is obviously not as healthy as it should be, the mind does not listen attentively to the heart's reactions, much less understand her. He may therefore pick up only vague impressions of the heart's experience of being dead-to-the-world or of self's non-existence. These impressions are translated by the mind as uncomfortable gut feelings, a vague uneasiness, a feeling of foreboding, or sometimes as merely a queasy stomach.

As the heart has her automatic response, so does the mind. As the masculine aspect of my consciousness, his response to facts is always to solve the literal problem, to make adjustments in the world. Though the heart's experience is illogical to the mind, he translates what he does pick up of her experience as just more outer facts. And having his own form of illogical logic — he calls it deductive reasoning — he's quite capable of responding to the heart's experience of being dead-to-the-world with the deduction, "Well, if I'm dead, then maybe I should abandon this body," as his logical solution. And the two of them will be of little help to each other as they have their first suicidal crisis. One woman reported that when her car broke down during a Between Lives period of her life, she felt overwhelmed with the task of getting something done about it, given her lack of ego-integration, energy, or motivation. "The thought crossed my mind that if I didn't have a body, I wouldn't need a car!" This, no doubt, was her mind's logical deductive reasoning and his idea of a helpful hint, which illustrates how easily suicidal "ideation" as a permanent solution to a temporary problem can be evoked in the BLS.

When Our Mind and Our Heart Are Lovers

The heart — our intuitive nature, our feminine self — is the mother of creativity. She creates out of an inner heartfelt need to nurture the seeds of heart-values. Her partner, the logical, intellectual, world-oriented mind, our masculine self, when in right relationship to his lover, is devoted to the heart's happiness. He kneels before her, holding her hand, attempting to discern her every desire. He then takes it as his happy mission to give life to her seed-values, to craft within the world those things that are the desires of the heart. He does this out of devotion to his lover and appreciation for her creativity. When in right relationship to his partner, he gives life to her heart-values, and his worldly life is informed by her values.

It is from within us then, that our new life will emerge as the love-child of these two inner lovers. And before the created thing emerges, the page in the outer world must necessarily be blank, the canvas bare. That is the outer pre-condition for creativity.

Our Dysfunctional Inner Family

At this current stage of our spiritual evolution, our mind/heart relationships are far from that ideal stage of maturity. They are in dire need of marriage counseling. We have not been aware that conscious communication and cooperation are possible between these two aspects of our consciousness and that a healthy relationship between them is crucial to our playing our role in life as responsible co-creators of our world. A haphazard creation is what results when the mind and heart do not take responsibility for consciously communicating and cooperating with each other in their creative roles.

Unfortunately, it rarely computes to our mind to consult our heart. In fact, he frequently squelches her desires aborning. He tends to become enchanted with the outer reality he sees and believes in as "facts of life." He is unaware that he has played a major role in projecting the picture he sees — by what he gave his attention and energy to. It is the immature mind's logical nature that surveys the outer world for us, looking for and never finding "out there" that mythical future — and then pronouncing it illogical to pursue things that are not (yet) visible. He reacts to the blank page, the bare canvas, with a distressed lament, "There's nothing out there to pursue," precipitating the heart's despair. The scariest factor about our current outer life ending is the lack of faith these two have in another life to come — though it surely will unfold, as day follows night.

The Future is Within Us

Of course, the next novel, career, identity, or life isn't "out there." It can only be "in here," waiting in the seeds of creative desire within our heart. We've become so enchanted with the movie playing out on the screen that we forget that our life is actually a projection, and that any change in the outer could much more easily occur from within the projector — our consciousness.

I remember hearing the story of a ranch hand who, many years ago, went to see his first movie, a Western "shoot-'em-up." He got so caught up in the story that in his excitement he suddenly jumped up, drew his gun, and fired several shots into the screen, to the amusement of the rest of the audience. To him, the story was out there and he was simply reacting to the disturbing outer circumstances. We laugh at him, but we are equally guilty of believing that the source of our life is "out there" and that we are at the mercy of those outer circumstances.

Our Most Important Craft Project

One of my chronically depressed clients reported to me that the only things in her life that didn't make her feel depressed were her craft projects. While she reacted to nearly everything else about her life with helplessness and depression, she loved to dream up new things to create. She enjoyed the process of finding the materials for creating them, and the challenge of revising her creative plan if not all the required materials could be found. After completing her project, if she didn't like it, she could toss it out with no regrets and dream up another project. "Nothing about my craft projects ever depresses me. Why can't I do that with my life?" she lamented.

Seeing that she knew how to be proactive toward crafts while limiting herself to simply reacting to life, I decided that she was onto something very important: the concept of treating one's life as one's most significant craft project. We worked together over the next few months to explore and develop this perspective. When perceiving her life from that viewpoint, she began to see how she had indeed created her life — by the choices she had made, and in some cases the choices she had refused to make that were therefore made by others with their own agendas. Abdication is also a choice, she found.

She also began to see the absurdity of feeling depressed helplessness as her reaction to what she herself had created. That was exactly like the ranch hand's response to the film on the screen: accepting outer circumstances as in control of her life from "out there," rather than recognizing her ability to change the circumstances at the source by changing the creative plan itself as she readily did with her craft projects. She knew that her craft projects originated in her mind/heart within her own consciousness. It was a revelation to discover that her very life did also.

Living her life as a craft project profoundly changed the way she felt about life, as well as changing how she lived it. For the first time in her life she began to feel a zest for living, and she found the courage to make some major changes. An important side effect was an end to her chronic depression. She made big changes in her world, eventually moving to another state and launching a new career. The following year she sent me a cartoon she had drawn that depicted her cartoon-self standing before a macramé wall hanging. Her cartoon-self had evidently crafted into the wall hanging a big knotty arm protruding from it, which had unexpectedly wrapped around her neck and was strangling her, to her obvious surprise. "This" she said, "is the life I had created for myself in the past. I thought I was at the mercy of my own craft project." How many of us are being strangled by our own self-crafted lives? How often do we react to circumstances with the helpless feeling that we're stuck with, and at the mercy of "the way things are"? If we learn to see our life as something we ourselves have crafted, we will also be able to see that we can change our life simply by making new choices, using the materials that life makes available to us.

4

The Tomb and The Womb: Coping with Two Stages of the BLS

The Between Lives experience that confronts us when some major phase of our life has ended, taking with it our world-connected ego-identity, can be divided into two main stages. The first is the Tomb stage and the second is that of the Womb.

The Tomb

The Tomb phase is our first experience of the Between Lives State and is that state into which we're catapulted immediately following the event that took away our most recent world-connected ego-identity. The most common symptoms experienced at first are shock and disorientation. We find it difficult to take in what has just happened, and cannot think beyond the confusing present moment. We may have a sense that nothing is as it was, but couldn't, if our life depended on it, imagine where we go from here. We know things are irrevocably changed, but we can't imagine beyond that.

Other symptoms of the Tomb stage appear to be our heart's natural, somewhat primitive, way of comforting our self in this circumstance of loss: numbness, sorrow, a slowing down of our mental processes, a desire to just be still without thinking or feeling, a reluctance or inability to think beyond the present moment.

Life's Demands

Our greatest problem in this chrysalis state is that we must still deal with the worldly problems that are difficult to handle, but now we face those challenges without the help of a well-integrated ego-identity. Few of the feelings we experience in the Tomb and Womb are of themselves unhealthy. The unhealthy factor is our lack of a safe cocoon to keep the world's demands at bay while we heal from our loss, sort ourselves out, and become wholly integrated again. Ordinary life does not recognize and respect our fragile status at this time; it still pursues us relentlessly with the need to seek employment, with divorce proceedings, with tax audits, bankruptcy proceedings, with eviction notices, flat tires, and a multitude of other stressful, energy-draining demands, at the same time requiring us to appear "normal" when that's the last thing we're feeling. This state of affairs raises the stress level exponentially, sometimes even precipitating a suicidal crisis, with the distressed mind presenting suicide as a "logical" alternative to dealing with the issue at hand. Such is the painful absurdity of this state of mind.

First Of All, Create Safety

During the initial Tomb stage, we must necessarily be preoccupied with finding protection, security, and nurturing for our changing self if we wish to have a relatively trauma-free transition. This is a cautionary period where it's not clear what will be, even in the near future. Since nature forgot to provide us with a safe cocoon for living through these vulnerable transitions, we must find a way to accomplish this for ourselves. We need a sanctuary for our soul, safe from invasion by worldly pressure, a quiet place where we can just "be," with no requirement that we be anything or anyone in particular. For we as a soul are entering a Time Out, a vacation from life, so that we can deal with the world while accepting the feeling of being "out of it," of being not really involved in life and not having the "heart" for participating in it.

Constructing a Time-Out Sanctuary

It would be very therapeutic, of course, if we could create such a place in the physical world where we could find real sanctuary, but we also need to create a virtual Time Out place on the mental plane where our thoughts can instantly take us, the moment worldly pressures threaten to cause a stress overload. Such a virtual sanctuary can save our life.

We can create our virtual sanctuary through a meditation exercise, where we enter our own secret garden. Within this safe place, we bring the things we've found nurturing in the past: a cabin by the ocean, perhaps, the scent of jasmine in the air, the soft purring of a contented cat, the crackling of a fireplace in winter, the cool green leaves of a potted fern, soft music, a view of a meadow covered with wildflowers — whatever we perceive to be nurturing to us personally. If we create such a mental sanctuary where we may retreat from worldly pressures at any moment, we will make survival through this period much less stressful.

This is an effective way for our conscious mind to soothe our distressed heart and keep control of our mental health, even while we live through this disconnected-from-life phase of life. It is a message to our subconscious — wherein originates all anxiety and stress — that we care about our self and will be there for our self as we trek through the valley of shadows of virtual death that lies between our past life and our future one.

Responsibility and Ability to Respond

A significant bonus of cooperating consciously with the processes involved in the Between Lives State is that the more problematic symptoms found there are subdued considerably by our ability to respond to them with a sane perspective. Those who don't consciously take responsibility for nurturing and protecting their soul while in the chrysalis state are much more vulnerable to the "survival behaviors" devised by their subconscious impressions, attitudes, and beliefs — the offspring of the mind and heart — which, for clarity's sake, I will personify as "inner children," who feel like orphans when we ignore our inner needs. It will not likely occur to us to take responsibility for our inner happiness until we see these aspects of our self as our inner children, needing nurturing, protection, and limits, like any other child. They "live" in the eternal Now of the heart, unaware of the concept of "future." The behaviors of these aspects of our consciousness are reflexive, and aim to solve the problem of the moment, with no perspective about future consequences. Quick fixes have the highest priority. The quicker the better, which is why drug and alcohol abuse are so popular among the world's inner kids! The brain gets an immediate message that "everything is ohkaaay!" and that's all the kids care about — feeling okay in this moment.

The orphaned inner kids are the culprits behind all violent acting out as well. If everyone in the world took to heart the saying, "Charity begins at home!" and attended first to the needs and welfare of their own inner kids, all "external" child abuse would vanish, all violence would be replaced by conflict resolution skills, and perhaps even war would be abandoned. The natural state of our "inner children" manifests as our happiness, joy, sense of fun, and contentment. When we ignore our inner welfare, the inner kids are the ones who eventually manifest physical illness, profound depression, nervous breakdowns, even suicide attempts. Everyone who has become aware of their inner kids in therapy sessions with me has sooner or later declared, "I don't want my inner kids running my life!"

These subconscious impressions, attitudes, and belief patterns that I personify as kids were never meant to run our life-in-the-world, and that's especially true during the chrysalis phase of life. Only our conscious mind has the ability to respond both to the heart within and to the worldly demands without. When we find ourselves in the BLS, the mind must say to the heart, "I don't know what's going to happen next. But I am committed to vigilantly protecting and caring for you throughout the entire process that's unfolding." When the heart feels cherished and protected it can endure anything. And the inner "kids" feel no need to take control. They are content to let the nurturing and protective "parents" remain in charge and perform their appropriate duties as "keepers of the soul."

Tasks of the Tomb Stage

The Tomb phase is a time of reflection, of making peace with the past, of getting closure and saying goodbye. Once we've established a safe and comforting sanctuary for our soul, when our consciousness feels a comfortable degree of security in this Between Lives State, and once we're past the shock, we can turn our attention to the major task of the Tomb stage. That task is to obtain closure on our most recent past life by reaching a healthy level of acceptance of its ending. It is during this process that we recognize the blessings we received during that phase of our life. We need to say goodbye to the people we leave behind, to the work we valued, to the places we loved, and to the person we were during that lifetime. Closure involves the processing of every significant facet of the past life that's ended and the leave-taking of our identity as we experienced our self in that life.

There is an ebb and flow to this process that seems to move more smoothly when we understand this and can just cooperate with whatever is happening at any given moment, without alarming ourselves with the fear that we're going in circles, continually backsliding, and that we'll never get beyond this. It is not, as it may seem, a vicious circle. Progress here takes the form of a spiral. We may repeatedly revisit and process the same things over and over again. But each time we come around again to an issue we had processed earlier, we always find ourselves at a higher level of understanding, acceptance, healing, and integration. It is helpful at this stage to have a support group who is willing to hear our story as many times as we need to tell it, for this hastens our adjustment, integration, and healing.

Getting Closure

The Tomb phase encompasses all the aspects of releasing the past to be the past, including appreciation for all the blessings it brought to us as well as satisfaction for the blessings we were able to bestow upon others.

It is crucial to our good health and adjustment to our future life that we do this processing thoroughly, that we finish all old unfinished business attached to our most recent past life. For if we don't feel finished, if we don't experience the healing of old wounds, if we don't get closure, then we don't let go. And we will carry this old weighty baggage with us into our next life, where it will surely color our attitudes and inevitably get projected onto and contaminate our new relationships and our new life.

Lessons from Past Lives

Another important task of the Tomb stage is to become aware of the lessons we learned in our just past life. Most of us who've established a new life after a major loss will admit that we are a different person now from the person we were in our past life. This transformation is a result of all the life-changing experiences that occurred during our last ego-life, culminating with the loss of that life itself. If we live our lives well, we're continually learning, growing, and changing. Generally, we're not aware of our own revisions of consciousness as they occur, because they are basically involved with the normal adjustments we're making to circumstances as life goes on from day to day.

But when an ego-life ends, our revised self, independent of its accustomed backdrop of that life, stands out in bold relief. It is then that we become aware of just how different we are from the person we were as a result of lessons learned in that past life. The most powerful lessons are those that not only change our minds but also transform our sense of self.

A Visit to Heaven and Hell

At this stage of the Between Lives State, it is possible to experience either hell or heaven or both, in turn, as we review our most recent past life from this detached viewpoint. If we weren't true to our highest self in that lifetime, then we may experience profound regret. Such remorse can be very helpful in resetting our priorities for our next life, with a vow to avoid making the same regretful mistakes again. Beyond that, remorse serves no useful purpose and should not be indulged in further.

On the positive side, we may also experience some level of bliss as we review those areas of our past life where we were true to our highest ideals, giving us a euphoric feeling of accomplishment. It is through this reviewing, judging, forgiving process that we obtain healing closure with our own past self.

Journal for Healing

A transitions journal is an effective and rewarding way to accomplish the task of getting closure regarding "unfinished business" — a gestalt therapy term referring to issues that stay in our mind/heart long after they should have and would have been put to rest, had we been able to resolve them at the time they occurred.

Conversing with the unforgotten issue is a way to deal effectively with our past in the present moment, the only time in which we can take action. The common belief is that we can't change the past, that it is forever frozen and unchanging. But we can definitely change our perceptions of it in the now. By bringing the old, unfinished issue into our present moment and confronting it in a dialogue, we can significantly alter our perceptions of the past, work through our hurt, anger, remorse — and move on from that place where we felt "stuck." Using this gestalt technique, we can effectively free ourselves from bondage to the past.

The Journaling Process

One easy way to use this gestalt technique is to write letters in our journal to the significant ones who will not be coming with us into our next life. We can tell them what we appreciated about them, what we still resent. We can pour out our love as well as our anger, hurt, and disappointment to them, letting it all come out to be released. It's therapeutic to tell it like it really is, not like it "should" be, telling them that we regret having them out of our life, or that we're glad they're gone, telling them of any resentment we may harbor that they left us so suddenly, creating so much trauma in our life. This is not the place for holding back politely. The more honest we can be in our journal, the greater will be our ultimate healing. It can feel good to complain in a letter to a departed spouse about his untimely death, "Look at the fine mess you've gotten us into!"

Letters from "The Other Side"

When we feel we've expressed to the departed the things that needed to be said, we should rest for a moment in our acceptance of the things we've written to him in our journal. Then we should read, from his viewpoint, what we have written. And, from that person's point of view, we should respond, telling his side of the story, speaking from that person's heart, allowing him to write a letter to us. It's important to continue back and forth with this written conversation until it feels finished, and there's nothing left to further disturb our heart.

We can use this method to get closure with any and every aspect of our past life, including our own past ego-identity, our past career, our past home — whatever must be left behind when we begin a new life. We can also request a message from each of them before we say goodbye, and allow them to write their message in our journal. It is amazing how healing this process is. This mental conversation can be a powerful tool for resolving the past and getting closure, taking us to a place where there's nothing left but love.

Gathering Up the Treasures

When we have worked through all our unfinished business with everyone and everything in our past life that seems significant to us, we can gather up the treasures that we've gleaned from those relationships — the patience and endurance we've developed; our healthier, more realistic perspective toward life; the love we've shared with others that has expanded our capacity to love; the memories of laughter and of tears; the expansion of our heart that comes from having experienced the sharing of life; the awareness we have now of life's possibilities that were unknown to us before that life; the experiences that have caused us to grow mentally and spiritually.

These precious jewels we now place in a treasure box, store them in our heart and take them with us as we cross the threshold into our soul's sanctuary once again. For these treasures will accompany us into our future life, blessings from a past life. How fortunate we are to be consciously aware that we carry such rich resources into our new life adventure.

Honor That Which is Dying

At this point, as we say our goodbye and prepare to close the door to our past life, we take a moment to honor that which is dying and that which is being born. We enter the chrysalis as one creature dying and emerge with renewed life, another creature entirely. It is difficult to believe it will happen. The caterpillar, I'm sure, had no such expectations either.

The Womb Stage of the BLS

There may be some overlapping between the Tomb and Womb phases. But in general, when we've reached some level of acceptance of and healing from our loss, and have processed most quarrels we may have had with the past, a very quiet period begins, in which the Womb phase of the BLS tends to unfold naturally. This phase of transition is usually marked by its rather peaceful, uneventful nature, with intermittent stirrings of new energy, much like any other gestation period.

Pamper the One "With Child"

During this phase of ego-transformation, take very seriously the advice of Proverbs: "Keep thy heart with all diligence, for out of it spring the issues of life."

This is a time when your mind should be preoccupied with the care and happiness of your heart, for the creation of your future life depends upon your heart's processes now. It's wise to start your day with a nurturing meditation period. Sarah Ban Breathnach's book, *Simple Abundance*, continues to be a recipe book for nurturing the heart while incubating a new life, conceived from the simple things in life that we appreciate. Reading a bit of it each morning is "food" for the heart.

Nurture Your Heart's Values

Our task in the Womb stage is to discover and nurture our heart's values — the things that make our heart happy and stir our enthusiasm — for these are the seeds of a new life. One way for your mind to entice these values to reveal themselves is to revisit deferred dreams, those desires that you may have shelved in your past life when events took you in another direction. In your journal start a list with the heading, "Something I've always wanted to do is ..." and add to the list whenever a new thought comes to mind. Don't allow practicality to censor these desires in any way, for that will squelch the flow. No matter how impractical it may seem to your skeptical mind to desire to sky-dive or climb Mount Everest, at least allow yourself to do it in your mind, and on paper. When your heart experiences unconditional acceptance of its dreams, she will become expansive and allow this all-important initial stage of the creative process to flow freely.

Another good technique for getting at your heart's values is to write the story of the rest of your life, seeing yourself doing whatever gives your heart pleasure, surrounded by the kinds of people you love to be with, in an environment that you would find nurturing, supportive and stimulating, doing the sort of work your hands and your mind enjoy. Remember that hearts, by nature, are not meant to be "practical." It is our mind's happy duty to find the practical application of our heart's dreams. There is always a way to craft our dreams, with modifications to fit the circumstances of the physical realm. When we consciously cooperate with this process, it speeds up considerably and is a source of pleasure, much like an enjoyable craft project.

Try On Hats

The Womb stage is an excellent time to try on many different hats, seeing how you like them. Working as a temp in many different fields can give you a taste of what it would be like to pursue careers in those fields, with very little investment of time and money on your part. Another way to check out possible new life activities is by taking college courses in subjects that intrigue you. A bonus of these strategies is that you are likely to find new friends there, an important ingredient of any new life.

Overcome Inertia

A vexing symptom of the BLS is the feeling of complete inertia, an inability to motivate yourself to move your body, not even toward activities that look interesting. This is a time for gentle discipline. You may have to be firm and use force to make yourself go register for a course, or apply for a job. It will not feel comfortable, or natural. It's said that "beginnings are apt to be shadowy." The initial stage of a new life may not feel like it could lead to anything good, for you are venturing into strange and unfamiliar territory.

It may take a huge effort of will to move your unwilling self toward new life. Remember that the first gear of an automobile is the most powerful, requiring the most fuel. That's because it has to overcome the inertia of the "stand-still state." This is the problem you are dealing with in yourself at the moment. If you can't persuade yourself to do it, just do it anyway. Give yourself permission to quit the activity in three weeks if you don't like it. But don't assume that waiting until you're willing to begin will work. Force yourself to move. Just do it. Despite the lack of faith you may have in this process, you will soon find yourself involved again in a new, interesting activity, and your energies will return to carry you onward smoothly. And you will have, without knowing just when, shifted into an easier gear.

Use Halfway Measures

Sometimes it pays to compromise with our unwilling self. In that case, halfway measures can serve us well. For instance, if we can't bring ourselves to apply for a job, even a temporary one, we might find it easier to take on a volunteer activity, which can restore our self-confidence and self-esteem.

Another halfway measure might be to audit an interesting class, if registering for credit seems too daunting. There is no pressure on you to "perform" to some academic standard when you audit a course. And as your interest rises, and your energies stir once again, you may soon find yourself looking forward to investing more of yourself in this direction by formally enrolling.

Whenever you come upon a stone wall of inertia and/or resistance within yourself concerning some activity that your mind has suggested moving toward, consider what a halfway measure would be, something that your unmoving body would be more willing to try. Halfway measures can be lifesavers in the Womb phase of the BLS.

In Summary

Basically, the major tasks of the Tomb and Womb phases of the chrysalis state are: creating safety for ourselves during this process of metamorphosis, getting closure regarding the past, integrating past-life lessons into our new, revised self and, based upon our new wisdom and perspective, conceiving and nurturing the birth of a new life expression and a new emerging ego-identity that connects us to a worldly life. When this cooperative work of our mind and heart is done, we happily enter our new life, and leave the symptoms of the valley of shadows behind in the BLS.

5

Survival Strategies: Helpful Hints for a Trek through the BLS

The moment we realize that we have lost our ego-identity and that we are between lives, we would be wise to become vigilant about our safety and care. Being proactive in taking responsibility for our welfare during this Time Out from a world-connected life can go a long way toward protecting us from the forty known side effects and symptoms of this temporary state.

Let me begin with an important caveat. When our life as we knew it has disappeared, we may get a strong "premonition" that the end of the world is very near. This belief is actually just a quirk of our subconscious mind as a result of the loss of our own personal world. But many people make foolish financial mistakes at this time based upon that feeling of impermanence of the world. These mistakes can profoundly affect their financial welfare in their future life — but they make them because they can't imagine that future life will ever manifest. A good rule to observe is to not make any drastic changes (unless absolutely necessary) — selling our home or business, relocating, moving in with relatives — for at least one year after the end of our most recent life. We may regain a realistic perspective sooner than that, but caution here can save us from future regret. If we must make changes, we should consult someone who can give us objective and expert advice.

Everyday Habits to Observe While in the BLS

When we are in the Between Lives State, it does not compute to our heart that we are alive, and she sometimes adjusts by putting the body into a hibernation mode. In such a case we must simulate active life until it begins again automatically. If you don't feel alive, consider how you would be acting if you did. Then "act as if" you were, as the AA saying goes.

The following are some suggested survival strategies:

- Breathe. When we feel dead to the world we sometimes forget to breathe. Our breathing becomes very shallow, which starves the cells of our body of needed oxygen, contributing to feelings of lethargy. Before leaving bed in the morning, take several slow, deep, cleansing breaths. With each conscious breath repeat a life-affirming thought, such as: "I breathe in the loving breath of Life." As you exhale, affirm some freeing statement such as, "I lovingly release that which is passing out of my life." Throughout the day remind yourself to breathe deeply.

- Move the body. Moving is another thing we forget to do when feeling dead to the world. Force yourself to take at least a ten-minute walk every day, in the fresh air, preferably — and breathe. Any gentle physical activity can give your subconscious the message that you are indeed still alive.

- Commune with Nature. Living flora and fauna, birds' songs, rippling water — these are serene messages of life to your heart, an inner reassurance of ever renewing

life. Our subconscious has a deep connection to Mother Nature, which underlies all life. Consciously connecting with Nature reaffirms our connection to life.
- Keep a rein on your attitudes. Control your attitudes so they don't control you. Assume that every child you ever were is still inside you, each manifesting as an attitude. Care for — and gently discipline — your attitudes like so many anxious children. Break the enchantment of being the child by seeing the child.
- Consider the source of absurd survival solutions. When our adult self feels powerless, it seems to the inner children that no adult is on duty, that they are abandoned orphans and must take charge, using their short-sighted survival skills that "solve" a problem in the present moment, but cause infinitely more problems in the future. "Future" is a concept that these inner kids cannot grasp, for they live in the heart, whose realm is the eternal Now. Assume that all toxic and/or ineffective nurturing and protective measures that come to mind are your inner kids' efforts at solutions. You will recognize their suggested solutions by their inadequacy, such as: Medicating feelings with abusive drugs; assaulting the problem-person; leaving the planet via suicide, etc. You can always recognize the kids' solutions because, while they have the appearance of solving a problem, they inevitably cause you more problems. Adult solutions, by definition, solve problems without causing more problems.
- Avoid melodrama. If you must go through bankruptcy, for instance, don't buy into the melodrama of it. Just be a detached observer as you go through the motions required for the proceedings. Tell your despairing, hysterical, or suicidal inner kids that it's not worth losing your health over. Stay in your self-made mental sanctuary and let

your automatic pilot go through the motions of the ordeal. Or contact your lawyer and let her handle it.
- Don't resist unavoidable disasters around you. When such disasters hit you, just let them wash over you, like ocean waves crashing upon a rock, while you remain non-resistant and detached. Remind your distressed inner kids, "This, too, shall pass." And promise your inner kids an "after-disaster" treat to look forward to if they will behave while your adult self does the work.

Take Good Care of Your Inner Children with Nurturing Activities

- Count at least five blessings morning and night. This attunes the inner kids to the blessings in your life and cultivates an attitude of gratitude that can help to counteract despair. A bonus is that it motivates your inner kids to look for blessings, and the positive energy inherent in such a search acts like a magnet within your consciousness for the inflow of even more blessings.
- Spend time daily nurturing your inner children.
  ◊ Serve yourself breakfast on a tray in bed.
  ◊ Read inspiring messages to yourself morning and night.
  ◊ Place mirrors where you'll see yourself often so that you realize that someone is here.
  ◊ Smile your support to this friend in the mirror. The soul behind this reflected personality is as important and vital to the universe as every other living soul on the planet.
- Keep to a healthy daily schedule of bathing, eating and sleeping. It affirms Divine Order for the inner kids. Since they live in the eternal Now, when their daily routine is

predictable, they believe that all is right with the world and they are not motivated to use their immature survival behaviors to solve their adults' problems.
- Put your inner children to bed with a comforting ritual. (If you awaken during the night, repeat the ritual.)
  ◊ Play healing music as lullabies for wooing sleep.
  ◊ See yourself handing over to God all your worries.
  ◊ Ask God to stay awake all night and take charge so you can get some sleep.
  ◊ See yourself surrounded by protective angels, and feel yourself soothed by nurturing ones.
  ◊ See yourself curled up comfortably in God's Hand.
  ◊ Surrender to God's infinite, loving presence.
- Treat despair like an inner child, sick with emotional nausea. Don't buy into the melodrama, but don't ignore the child. A cool cloth on the forehead, a cup of peppermint tea, the feeling that you care can be very soothing for such nausea. Don't allow this child to indulge in despairing thoughts. The imagination is not a toy and inner kids should not be playing around with it, especially when they're feeling sick with despair.
- Write your thoughts, feelings and experiences in a Between Lives journal. The journaling I discussed in the previous chapter can be expanded here to intentionally include your inner kids. Write in the date of each entry, so that when you review it later, you'll see the progress you've made over time. This helps to reestablish perspective. See your journal as a friend with whom you can share your experiences and feelings. Ask your past life if it has any advice for you. Write down the response. Invite your inner kids to write their complaint to God in your journal.

Then listen with your heart for God's response and write it down also.

- Write down a list of thirty things, large and small, that you'd like to do before you leave the planet, getting input from your inner kids. Read this list to them weekly. Determine which of these goals you can move toward now, at least in some modest way. Make a "treasure map" collage depicting the things on your list. Images are the heart's language. This forges a link with a future life.

More Strategies: Perspective, Vacation, Support

- Put your problems into perspective. In your mind, zoom into the future ten years from now, and from that vantage point look back upon this time in your life. Does your future self see your current problems as just a time for needed adjustment, or are they heralding the end of this phase of your life? Ask your future self for some advice on how to handle your current dilemmas. Write the responses in your journal. Ask your future self if your current problems are meant to teach you lessons, or are they actually blessings in disguise. Ask your future self for his/her help in dealing with the present, and be open to receiving.

- Get into a "vacation" mode. Since the BLS is a vacation of sorts — a Time Out from normal life — treat yourself to all the special things that you would normally reserve for vacations, such as:
    ◊ Take up a new hobby.
    ◊ Take an art class.
    ◊ Go on a retreat.

- ◊ Learn a new skill.
- ◊ Build something.
- ◊ Read a novel.
- Create a Life Transitions support group for yourself. Since well-meaning friends and family often have difficulty empathizing with our between lives symptoms, we need people who can. Consider starting a Life Transitions support group for others in the BLS. If possible, ask a therapist friend — or maybe just a therapeutic friend — to join you in this project. Your library or recreation center may have free space your group can use for a couple of hours every week. Post flyers inviting people who are in transitions to join you. Participants in such a group who learn about the BLS have fewer symptoms, avoid the more serious symptoms altogether, and tend to enter new lives within four to six months, compared to the twelve to eighteen months that others spend wandering around the valley of shadows before stumbling into a new life. Group members are always surprised by the laughter — it's the first time some of them have laughed since the end of their most recent past life.

The investment you make in proactively caring for yourself while in the Between Lives State will pay off significantly, preventing the manifestation of the more distressing symptoms. Being vigilant about your emotional safety, giving loving attention to yourself, and creating a caring support system for yourself will minimize the discomfort involved in the loss of your world-connected ego-identity. And nurturing your creativity will hasten the birth of your next life-expression, and will take you happily out of the BLS and into normal life in the world again, where you can live your next chapter as a freshly revised creature of the universe.

6

Enchantments: Getting Stuck in the BLS

While most of us do make it through the BLS and go on to live rich lives once again, some people suffer its symptoms as a chronic condition because they get stuck in the morass of the Between Lives State and are unable to move through it. It is as if they have fallen under a spell, an enchantment, that prevents them from seeing the reality of their situation.

Enchantments

We may have thought that enchantments were magical fictions of fairy tales. But in my work, I have found many people who were caught in enchantments, often staying psychologically frozen in a certain age bracket or role, unable to think in any other way, and unaware that they were indeed stuck in a mindset that prevented them from living a more authentic and satisfying life. The following are extreme cases that illustrate the point. These people are caught in various forms of enchantment that keep them from entering fully into life and are therefore vulnerable to all the symptoms of the BLS.

Always the Bride

When I was a child, I heard the story of a bride whose groom was killed on the way to their wedding. Unable to accept this horrible turn of events, she had a nervous breakdown and was hospitalized. The story goes that she spent years in a mental institution, continually packing and unpacking her trousseau, oblivious to life around her. This woman stayed firmly entrenched in that moment before life took an unexpected drastic turn. Unable to make the turn, she was stuck in the last moments before the unacceptable life change. No one was able to penetrate the insulated bubble in which she protected herself from the tragic facts of her life. Some part of her consciousness held her hostage to the happy dream rather than face and deal with the pain of the truth that could have invited eventual healing and movement toward new, happy life experiences.

Getting Stuck at the Hairpin Curve

Sometimes a wholly unexpected turn in the road can so throw a person — especially those who aren't able to take corners very swiftly — that they stop dead in their tracks, unable to go on, because "going on," to them, can only mean continuing on the same track they were on. But the surprise turn that life events took erased that life-track and, in effect, destroyed life as they knew it.

Their rationale for being what I label "stuck", or enchanted, would be that they are waiting right where life got off its track, until it rights itself again; then they can proceed with their life once more. That feels sane to them. They are enchanted with the belief that their original track was life and that what's happened since then is not.

Missing the Turn in the Road

My friend Sue's childhood pal, Marilyn, came to visit her from Seattle. They had skated through the city and enjoyed their childhood together. Now they were both twenty-five, and while Sue looked her age, Marilyn looked like a twelve-year-old. She dressed like a twelve-year-old and styled her hair like one. She had the lifestyle of an adolescent and seemed to be drifting through life without meaning or direction. On a hunch, I asked Sue what had happened to Marilyn when she was twelve. She told me, "Her parents suddenly, without warning, sent her away to a boarding school and got a divorce. She really flipped out, and walked around in shock for a long time." It was obvious to me that she was still walking around in shock.

Getting "Stuck" in a State of Shock

Shock is one of the first symptoms of the Between Lives State for most of us when confronted by sudden and unexpected change. But for a few, it becomes a permanent state of enchantment, and they hang suspended in time. If their plight goes unrecognized and they don't receive help in adjusting, some people can stay stuck for a very long time, unable to pick up the pieces and create a new life with the new materials life has handed them.

Before her parents' divorce, Marilyn had no doubt been under the impression that life with her family would continue as it was until she was grown. The first major turn in the road of life would be her own leave-taking for college, seemingly far in the future to a twelve-year-old. So the sudden surprise move to a boarding school at twelve, coupled with her parents' unexpected breakup of the family, shattered her perception of everything she had known as life. Marilyn had determinedly remained as she was when she was twelve. That was to her, evidently, the only sane ground she had to stand on.

Awakening from Enchantments

Helping a person stuck between lives requires meeting her where she is and assisting her in a step-by-step process of reviewing her life up to and through the moment her life-pattern was disrupted. Awakening from the enchantment requires making the connections between the "before" and "after" lives. Such an awakening should not be forced even if possible. To have this stable ground pulled out from under her before she sees another sane place to stand could have aversive effects. Clinging firmly to its last known "reality" is just one of the mind's ways of protecting itself when no other reality seems possible. But such myopia causes a few other problems.

The Homeless

Approximately 600,000 Americans are homeless on any given night. Those who are among the chronic homeless are perhaps the most easily recognizable people stuck between lives. Somehow their connection to what we'd call normal life has been broken, and they've not found a way to become reestablished in such a life again.

The Mentally Ill

An estimated one-third of the chronic homeless have a history of mental illness. When advances in psychotropic medications allowed such people to function more or less adequately without hospitalization, institutional care for the mentally ill lost favor. It was believed that they could be adequately supported in their communities by newly established mental health clinics and ongoing use of effective medications. Unfortunately, there was no way for the mental health clinics to require these patients to keep scheduled appointments. And without someone watching over them, many discontinued their medications, that being the crucial factor that could possibly have enabled them to live fairly normal lives, keeping a steady job and establishing a home. There was never any nationally organized effort to realistically create the supportive community these people required. Lacking the necessary ego-integration to establish and support themselves on their own, and neglected by the unaware community, the homeless mentally ill have done the best they could under the circumstances. These fragile people cannot, without ongoing community support, maintain a life, and thus they stay stuck between lives, often wandering from pillar to post in a non-living state.

War Veterans

Another significant population of homeless people throughout history have been veterans of wars. From the earliest civilizations until today, young men left their homes as patriotic teenagers and were subjected to experiences that were foreign to everything they'd learned up until then. In many cases, these experiences so changed them that, after the war, they could not pick up their old identities and return to their former lives, nor find a new place in society again. Some never really do adjust, and remain stuck between lives.

One doesn't have to be a veteran nor mentally ill in order to become homeless. There are many causes for homelessness in our country. But the homeless all share a common attribute: They all somehow have lost their places as participants in the society that we consider the norm. No matter what misfortune got them there, the homeless in America find many barriers to reestablishing themselves in a normal life again. In many cases, being homeless is enough to keep them homeless. And they may experience all the symptoms of the BLS.

Those Who are Rudely Awakened from the American Dream

Since just after World War II, Americans have been enchanted with a fantasy known as "the American Dream." Through hard work, the dream goes, we will be successful, have it all, and live happily ever after. In his book, *The Good Life and its Discontents*, Robert Samuelson has explored this romance we have had with the dream of perpetual success. Unfortunately, according to him, the fantasy became expectation. If we "play by the rules," we expect that success will be our reward.

Dreams seldom come with caveats. When we built our dream houses, we didn't visualize them sliding downhill in an unscheduled mudslide, nor soaking in the waters of an overflowing river, nor being demolished by the ruthless whirls of a sudden tornado. When we built our families, we never visualized their disintegration through the dissolution of our marriages. And when we "played by the rules" and gave loyal service to one company for a lifetime, we never visualized a new management changing the rules and choosing to "downsize" us just before our pensioned retirement was due.

When such events jolt us from our dream-state and disrupt our expectations, we tend to feel, not only severely disappointed, but deeply betrayed. We may even lose trust in life, and in ourselves. This disruption of the American Dream can lead to profound disillusionment and precipitate all the symptoms of the Between Lives State. Furthermore, if we cannot adjust to the changed rules and the changed world to create a new, realistic dream and a new life, we may stay stuck in the BLS for the rest of our lives.

Stuck in a State of Mind

Some people get thrown into the BLS through unexpected life circumstances. But it is often the makeup of their consciousness that causes them to stay stuck in this non-living state. The following are a few forms that the idealist — and especially the dysfunctional idealist — mindset can take and that can keep a person trapped in the Between Lives State.

Dysfunctional Idealists

Idealism is good. Dysfunctional idealism is not. For it is misplaced and inappropriate idealism that, at the least, causes the dysfunctional idealist to experience chronic disappointment, and at the worst, can lead to crimes against humanity.

Dysfunctional idealism is an enchantment that warps the dysfunctional idealist's perspective and therefore adversely affects his entire life, including all his relationships. Many dysfunctional idealists stay stuck between lives because they are prepared to live only the ideal, but their version of the ideal is just not happening "out there" in the world. All of us may cling to some form of unrealistic idealism in some area of our lives without undue adverse effect. It becomes dysfunctional when it interferes with our ability to accept the world in which we live and deal with it realistically, when it renders us powerless to maintain a happy life, or when we believe it is our duty to impose our perception of the rules of life upon others, denying them their right to follow the dictates of their own consciences. Dysfunctional idealism can cause us to be chronically frustrated, depressed, angered, and in extreme cases even murderous or suicidal. Prejudice is a toxic form of dysfunctional idealism. Religion has been blamed for many of humanity's worst deeds. But a closer look will reveal the culprit to be dysfunctional idealism wrapped in the cloak of religion. It's as if the founders of religions have been taken hostage by dysfunctional idealists.

A characteristic of dysfunctional idealism is adhering tenaciously to an idealistic belief system based upon some information taken in uncritically in the past — often tainted with wishful thinking — and subsequently set in concrete as a "given" that we never consciously think to question, though it proves to be distorted or inaccurate time and again. It can take the form of romantic or fatalistic thinking. It may embrace the belief that righteousness has the right-of-way because it should have the right-of-way! It can convince us that there are ironclad universal rules and that we know what those rules are for everyone and every circumstance. It may take the form of an enchantment of external locus of control — the romance of suffering and of being victimized. Sometimes it is an enchantment of being a savior of others, or of being the keeper and enforcer of "The Rules."

All dysfunctional idealism is misplaced and, therefore, inappropriate idealism; it is non-responsive to reality. We may tenaciously believe in the truth of a thing because we very much want it to be true, not because we have any evidence that it is. This is a childlike mode of magical thinking that requires the suspension of logical reason. There is often an element of self-righteousness, and sometimes rigid immaturity, involved in dysfunctional idealism. These limited, delusional thought patterns can persist all our lives if we never consciously revise our thinking. Some people literally ruin their lives with willfully unrealistic attitudes and resultant behavior patterns so at odds with reality that they cannot function effectively in the world.

There is a great resistance to giving up this affliction because it initially feels good. It feels righteous. It allows us at times to dwell in a state of euphoria, which can become a psychological drug addiction. When this pattern of thinking leads to the inevitable disappointments, the dysfunctional idealist never "gets it" — never sees that the flaw is in his own thinking. His reaction to the disappointment can be either depression, anger, righteous indignation, or all three at once. Many dysfunctional idealists get so depressed they become suicidal. Others feel rage, and may take on the role of enforcer of the rules. In such a case, their zeal can sometimes lead to violent drastic actions.

Some of humanity's most heinous atrocities were committed in the name of idealism. The driving force behind the insanity and horror of Nazism was the ideal of creating a master race. Cambodia's Pol Pot had a dream of returning his countrymen to a simpler way of life, and this ideal led to the deliberate murder of at least two million Cambodians — those educated citizens who might resist his mission.

Terrorist attacks occurring around the world today are fueled by dysfunctional idealism. Timothy McVeigh blew up a federal building in retaliation for the Waco debacle caused by his perceptions of government agencies mishandling the hostage situation at the Branch Davidian compound in the early 1990s. He was justified in his actions, he insisted while on Death Row, because he had declared war on the American government. And the killing of the children in the childcare center there was regrettable, he said, but it was "collateral damage" of war. In September of 2001, suicidal terrorists hijacked airliners and crashed them into the World Trade Center buildings in New York City and into the Pentagon building in Washington, DC, killing thousands, and awakening America to the diabolical threat that virulent dysfunctional idealism, cloaked in religion, poses to their nation and to the world. These extreme cases illustrate the darkest side of dysfunctional idealism. The desire to impose one's beliefs and prejudices upon others is the mother of many evil acts in the world.

The poisonous nature of dysfunctional idealism can be found embedded in every culture of the world, including America's. One of my spiritual teachers advised, "If you would find your most insidious vices, look behind your virtues." The virtue of idealism can conceal deeply embedded prejudices. A leader of America's so-called "religious right" revealed prejudices cloaked in religion in remarking, at the time of the WTC and Pentagon bombings, that God had allowed terrorists to attack America because of the work of civil liberties groups, abortion rights supporters, and feminists.

In oppressive forms of manmade religion, it becomes a virtue to adamantly ignore facts in favor of blind faith, restricting the faithful one to unexamined dogma as his reality. And the misuse of God for enforcing one's own version of what's "right" seems to be a common human frailty. A New Yorker cartoon illustrated this point, showing a mother and small son sitting at a kitchen table during a severe thunderstorm, with huge bolts of lightning flashing outside the window. The mother is saying to the son, "That's just God's way of saying, 'Why don't you eat your carrots?'"

The Terminal Idealist

The final psychological stage of dysfunctional idealism, when carried to its inevitable conclusion, eventually leads to profound disillusionment. At this point, the dysfunctional idealist often retreats from the world, nursing feelings of disgust and cynicism. People call them "curmudgeons." They are not happy people.

Breaking the Enchantment

The most effective solution to this malady is to embrace "recovering idealism." A person who adopts this attitude continues to cherish idealism, but at the same time persistently deals with outer facts realistically, and strictly avoids wishful thinking. One recovering idealist told me that, in a despairing moment, she was close to suicide, saying mournfully to herself, "I won't live in a world where people are not motivated by love!" At that low point, she heard an inner voice calmly respond, saying, "Perhaps 'love' is not the theme that God is working on at the moment." It was as though someone had thrown ice water in her face, she said. "It had never occurred to me that my idea of a loving world might just have to go through some preliminary stages first." Who knows? Perhaps a just world must come before universal love can be made manifest. At that point, she realized that she had better leave it to God to micromanage the world, and limit her own activities to creating as loving a personal environment as she could. Former president Lyndon Johnson, who was a very practical idealist, was known to say, "If you can't do the impossible, do the possible," — very good advice to idealists. This strategy requires dealing with the facts, and putting wishful thinking in its place.

Spiritual Aspirants

For many years, I've lived near a spiritual retreat and have been a counselor/therapist to many spiritual aspirants, another group of people who can stay stuck between lives because of their value systems. They tend to not value what worldly people value. They have little worldly ambition, and find it difficult to maintain the necessary level of energy and drive required to participate fully in the workaday world. Associating with world-oriented people can accentuate their feelings of alienation, an experience shared by others in the BLS.

The most natural way for spiritual aspirants to connect with worldly life is to be here for God's reasons — through service, doing the work that would please God. Whatever connection they can make to life in the world will protect them from the BLS symptoms.

The Misunderstanding World

It's important to remember that people who are firmly established in their own lives do not understand this Between Lives phenomenon when they behold someone whose "reality" has disappeared. They may even be resistant to understanding it because doing so would mean acknowledging that their own reality is similarly fragile, and the idea of their own fragility could cause them great stress. Thus, they tend to attribute Between Lives behaviors to other causes, such as laziness, moral turpitude, mental illness, or anti-social contrariness. They don't know of the paralysis that sets in when the BLS person experiences himself as "dead to the world," when his connection to his life has gone. Therefore, world-connected people often have little patience or sympathy for those who are thus afflicted. Tentative attempts to rescue through "quick fixes" never work. They just end up frustrating and irritating the would-be rescuer, often causing a cold and heartless reaction, whereby they exhort the hapless person to just "snap out of it" or "get over it," thus pushing the afflicted ones even further into alienation and isolation, and exacerbating their problems.

Understanding the nature of this Between Lives State will lead to compassion for those who have become stuck there. A compassionate response to their dilemma can alleviate their isolation and perhaps even break the enchantment in which they may be caught.

7

Helping Teenagers Survive the BLS of Adolescence

My experience with adolescents is extensive. My own four children were so close in age that during a seven-year period there were always three teenagers in our household at the same time. And over a period of twenty-five years, I have worked with scores of at-risk adolescents in six residential treatment programs.

We've all endured adolescence, a period of time that is one long Between Lives State. During those teenage years we struggled to cope with life, with little to help us but our fragile and ever-changing self-concept. No longer possessing the familiar ego-identity of "child," but not yet safely connected to that of the purposeful, self-assured "adult," we suffered through most of the forty symptoms of the BLS, running the gamut from disorientation to active suicidal crisis.

As teenagers, we experienced ourselves as powerless to control any facet of our lives. Nor did we own even the ground we stood on, a fact that our distraught parents sometimes pointed out to us ("This is my house, and as long as you're under my roof you'll follow my rules!"). If our parents decided to move to a desert island, we found ourselves on a desert island, without any inner connection to that new reality. The decision to move was not based on our adolescent values, nor were we likely even to have been consulted or given a choice. Another common experience, and equally disintegrating, was shared by those of us whose parents divorced. We felt jerked around by outer circumstances that were not in our control, and were not happening for any reasons of our own. Our lives were often disintegrated by these outer forces, and they created a trauma similar to those of a displaced person whose entire world was bombed out of existence during war. At-risk adolescents display many of the symptoms of post-traumatic stress disorder and most of the problems experienced by war refugees. In recent years, some judges have begun mandating an innovative "visitation" policy, (aptly referred to as 'bird-nesting') in which the children of a divorcing couple remain in the family home, and it is the parents who move in and out, in turn, to be with their children there. The fact that many people find this idea startling reveals how little we have empathized with the child when his life is totally disrupted for the parents' convenience after a divorce.

A Population at Risk

It shouldn't be surprising that a teen might experience suicidal feelings at some time during this long, disintegrated, chrysalis phase of life. Caterpillars are provided cocoons to help them endure this transformational process, during which they become something akin to raw scrambled eggs before they're put back together again as completely different creatures — beautiful winged butterflies. Unfortunately, adolescence is one unrelenting Between Lives State without the benefit of a safe Time Out cocoon. For years on end, a teen's self-concept is fragile, fragmented, distorted, and in constant flux. And most have no real vision of a future to focus on, or even believe in, that would help them keep their balance. It's the perfect set-up for experiencing any and all of the Between Lives symptoms.

Adolescents Get No Respect

Recently, I was riding with a friend in her car, her two teen-aged sons in the back seat. My friend suddenly looked in the rear-view mirror and asked them, "Did you change your underwear?" I was appalled and extremely embarrassed. Surely her sons were, too. No adult would ask this question of another adult. But it doesn't occur to many parents to extend to their children the respect, or even the courtesy, that they automatically give to other people. Treating a child with respect sends the message that he is a valued and esteemed person, and goes a long way toward building healthy self-esteem and self-confidence.

Non-Persons in Limbo

Furthermore, our culture has evolved in such a way as to deny any meaningful role for adolescents to play that could give their adolescent life meaning and purpose along with a life-connected identity. Currently, children in America are treated much like pets, whose care must be arranged for while the adults are away. These children are given no responsibility to contribute to the family's welfare — even though such responsibility could give them dignity and purpose along with "roots" in their life. They are baby-sat until old enough to stay alone, and they're kept busy or else pretty much left to their own devices after they reach pre-adolescence. Surveys have found that those hours after school and before parents arrive home from work are the hours when most teen experimentation with sex and drugs occurs. The main reason given for these activities is: "Nothing else to do."

Child labor laws were rightfully created to prevent the exploitation of children. But there must be some meaningful family and community roles that adolescents could play in that vast area between the extremes of exploitation on the one hand and the shelving of a generation on the other. So far, the only role adolescents have been given in American society is that of consumer, a role bestowed upon them by the avaricious advertising community and funded by their overworked parents. Too many parents are (or think they are) incapable of providing their children with their time, their interested attention, or with meaningful connections to family and community life. If parents can give little energy to their children except in the form of money, they can expect their children to be bought by those who want to exploit this easy target market. Some of these overextended and exhausted parents inadvertently leave to the media the task of instilling values and a sense of self into their offspring. The parents' unease about their child's welfare in today's society is assuaged by the fact that they can see their child is safely seated in his room with his television and/or computer to keep him occupied and off the streets.

But the media feel no sense of responsibility for the task of instilling healthy values, or for appropriately socializing this audience. They just want the kids' money. In fact, pre-adolescents and adolescents are considered such a lucrative market that in 2019 close to 5 billion dollars was spent on advertising targeting children. In addition to the dollars that can be tracked, there is the ubiquitous stealth advertising across social media that is very difficult to quantify, but that is a type of ubiquitous advertising to which children are even more susceptible than they are to more overt types of messages.

Additionally, most parents don't realize that the computer games that emphasize "search and destroy" are the same sort of tools used by the military to desensitize soldiers to the act of mass killing. They are designed to make killing acceptable to the players, to make it an automatic response of their subconscious, a "game" — thus making them more willing to become killing machines when in combat. These games are known to have been used by many of the adolescents who later became killing machines themselves. Their parents may have looked in on them and seen them sitting quietly in front of their computers, fully concentrating on its screen, for all the world looking like happy, well-adjusted people, at peace and safe from the dangerous world, not causing their parents any concern. The following example (fictionalized here to protect privacy) illustrates one adolescent's "between lives" perspective.

One Adolescent's Story

Jan was brought to counseling by her mother. This red-headed teenager was obviously hostile to the idea of talking to a counselor, but her mother was anxiously insisting that she come. She looked like a person with her mind determinedly closed. At the first opportunity she stormed out of my office, to her mother's dismay, though I wasn't surprised. It's not really possible to impose counseling upon anyone against their will. But this gave me an opportunity to talk with her mother and to get their story from her perspective. Jan's mother reported that she and her husband had been at war since their first year of marriage. Through all the difficult years of living in her parents' stormy marriage, Jan had somehow managed to be a happy, well-adjusted "A" student. Then when she was fourteen, Jan's parents divorced, and mother and daughter moved to another town. Her mother looked forward to establishing a more peaceful home life for Jan and herself. But to her confusion, now that Jan's new environment was free of strife, she was flunking out in her new high school. She regularly skipped school and hung out with the "fringe" kids, the dropouts involved in drugs and promiscuity. When her mother tried to express her concern, Jan would storm out of the house and sometimes not come home all night. Her mother was beside herself with worry for her daughter's safety, as she suspected Jan was involved in other dangerous behaviors.

A few weeks after that interview, Jan and her friends were

arrested and charged with drug possession and trespassing. Since Jan's involvement was marginal, the judge gave her probation and remanded her to the custody of her mother on the condition that she receive counseling. So Jan reluctantly returned to my office. It took a while, but I eventually gained her trust as the "lawyer for her happiness." Jan's risky behavior was very new to her. And the truth was, Jan herself couldn't say why she was doing what she was doing. She was severely depressed, and felt no motivation to excel in school any more. Everything had lost its meaning.

Lost Identity

Jan's basic problem was that she was having feelings similar to those that many displaced people experience during wartime, when their entire hometown has been destroyed, and there is no familiar landmark left to help the survivors get their bearings or reclaim their former identities. The haunted expressions on the faces of people displaced by war isn't caused solely by the horrors they've seen, but also by the disappearance of their own lives and sense of self, lost forever in the rubble.

When Jan's mother's life in her marriage ended, she instinctively went back to the roots of her own life — her old hometown. Whether through death or divorce, when a marriage ends, we often return psychologically to where we'd left off our former life. We may, for a time, experience being the age and the personality we were just before we'd entered that relationship years ago, an experience that can be very confusing if we're not aware of this psychological quirk of our subconscious processes. Our heart's memory is triggered by association, and "takes us back" to a similar experience from our past. It's the same memory mode that, upon hearing an old love song, transports us instantly to another time and place in our life as if it were happening now. "Flashback" is one of the Right Mind's — or heart's — memory modes. If, after a twenty-five year marriage ends, we find ourselves being twenty years old again, it's our heart returning us in memory to the place where we left off being single.

This move "back home" was no doubt a psychologically logical thing for Jan's mother to do for herself. Its purpose was to help her pick up the threads of her identity as a single person and get on with the process of creating a new life. But for Jan it was devastating, for her world as she knew it had disappeared. Her parents' marriage, which had been her safe home base, was now gone. Her school, her teachers, her daily routine in a familiar environment was gone. Her friends who had known her since first grade in school, the familiar world of her hometown — all were gone from her life, taking her budding adolescent identity with them. The Jan that she knew, her identity in that world, her perceptions of what her life was about had been shattered and no longer existed for her.

Lost Trust

Further, Jan's trust of life had been shattered. How could she pursue academic goals that had disappeared into thin air, along with her familiar world and her identity? In the past, she was getting to know who she was and where she was headed. But this move to an unfamiliar town and an unfamiliar school, populated with strangers who did not reflect back to her any image of herself with which she was familiar, had destroyed her assumptions about life and shattered her already fragile adolescent concept of self. None of her previous goals made sense to her now, for they were based upon her beliefs about who she'd thought herself to be and what her life was and would become — all now gone. Yes, life at home was more peaceful now, but it wasn't her life; it wasn't her home. She had literally lost her life.

Adolescent Survival Mode

Suicidal thoughts cross the minds of adolescents when they feel they can't take the pressure of functioning in a world where they do not have a meaningful role, a living connection. For this reason, doing drugs can seem like a viable "half-way measure" to them, not as serious as the suicide they've been considering. Sexual promiscuity doesn't seem very important either if they don't see themselves living very long anyway. And the future doesn't exist for them, so future consequences for these behaviors don't exist either. Sex and drugs are two primal survival behaviors that give comfort and surcease in the present moment, the only time the at-risk adolescent really can believe in. They hang out with the "fringe kids" because these, too, are "lost souls," unable to connect to life in a meaningful way. It is their support group. Their affiliation with other people similarly disenfranchised is their way of meeting their very real need for a support system in their alienated state.

Someone recently characterized this phase of life as "the valley of shadows of adolescence," a darkly apt description of the phase of life where we have left childhood behind, but have not yet developed the consciousness of nor capacity to be an adult. During these years we dwell in a surrealistic world with no relevant past experience we can apply to give us perspective, no effective behaviors to cope with the serious adult problems that are beginning to confront us, and no hope to sustain us.

Suicide Risk among Teenagers

Suicide is an important cause of mortality among youths in the United States. The Centers for Disease Control and Prevention (CDC) reported that the rates of suicide among young people increased 56% between 2007 and 2016. In 2017 the National Institute of Mental Health listed it as the second leading cause of death for youth 10–14 years of age as well as those aged 15–24.

2018 statistics from the CDC reveal that in 2017, the percentage of high school students who reported that they had thought seriously about committing suicide reached a startling 17 percent, while 13.6 percent had made a plan, and 9 percent had attempted suicide. Among adolescents suffering from depression the rate of suicidal ideation was estimated to be as high as 40 to 50 percent. Females were almost twice as likely as males to be at risk for suicide attempts, but males were more likely to succeed in that tragic act.

With such a high number of students — 9 percent in the CDC report mentioned — acting out their despair by attempting suicide, we can be sure that very many more adolescents experience painful suicidal feelings without acting on them.

The Adolescent's Perspective

Adolescents are very unlikely to bring any reasonable perspective to their condition. As is perfectly normal for their stage of development, they have precious little of it. If a relationship ends, they think the world has ended; if they fail an exam, they think they've flunked out of life. In short, if some distorted illusion about life proves false, they think that life has proven false. And the lack of life experience deprives them of memories of better times that could help them hold on to hope until something new and better develops. Teenagers in general do not experience hope, for the concept of hope presupposes a future, and they typically can visualize no future that contains them. The fact is, their current caterpillar-self will not be entering the future. It will be their future butterfly-self, with whom they in no way identify, who will live in that future life.

To complicate matters, some personalities, like Jan's, are more fixed or rigid, less flexible than others. They take longer to make up their minds and after they do, they are very resistant to changing them. These souls are often accused of being stubborn, when in fact they are just responding to sudden change in the only way that seems sane to them — with the attitude that if they just stand still, the world will stop its dizzying gyrations. The development of these inflexible personalities can be seriously disrupted by sudden life changes, such as parental divorce or death, relocating to a new community, or anything that changes the apparent direction of their lives more or less suddenly and more or less permanently. Any ego-identity that they'd developed up to that point may be held to tenaciously, because to them that's the only sane thing to do until the world stops spinning out of control and gets back to "normal," that is, gets back to the condition they'd come to believe was "the way the world is."

For such adolescents, their adjustment to life can be permanently shattered by these unexpected turns in the road. They just cannot make the turn, basically because it doesn't occur to them that it is they who must do the changing. Their belief is that life is the factor that somehow got off track, and they feel quite powerless in the situation.

Getting Back On Track

The easiest way to facilitate Jan's needed adjustment of attitudes and behaviors would be, first of all, to help her parents understand her perspective. Also, it would be helpful for her to participate in individual therapy — or better still, a peer support group. There she could gain perspective regarding the changes she'd experienced, get in touch with her core beliefs, and explore her options, all for the purpose of reestablishing a concept of herself that could once again connect her to an ongoing life-script. This is about perspective. She could only adjust to life when life made sense to her. Her current at-risk behaviors were indeed her adjustment to her current perceptions of life as chaotic, meaningless, not within her control, and leading toward nothing.

Finding Identity through Others

It often helps an at-risk adolescent to involve herself in volunteer work with both small children and the elderly, at pre-schools and nursing homes. Working with the elderly gives her the benefits of relating to an older generation and helps her make a connection with the natural ongoing patterns of life, a perspective denied many adolescents in their insular existences. And working with very young children has a similar effect. It also evokes an adult from within, along with feelings of compassion, responsibility, and purpose. It facilitates the development of a vision of themselves as future parents and of a future life in general, with purpose and meaning — a vision sorely lacking in the consciousness of most at-risk adolescents.

Helping those who are even more vulnerable than she will tend to strengthen her self-esteem and promote a more positive and realistic perspective. The love and appreciation she receives from the children and the elders will be a nurturing connection for her heart.

Staying Life-Oriented

Adolescents, in order to stay life-oriented, need to have:

- A safe, pressure-free sanctuary of their own.
- A sense of belonging.
- A sense of connection to life.
- A sense of connection to community.
- An emotional connection to others.
- A sense that their life has meaning and worth.
- A sense of continuity.
- A meaningful role in dealing with sudden, unavoidable life disruptions.
- Someone who they believe understands their viewpoint.

During this long transitional BLS phase called adolescence, it's important that the teenager employ every means possible to remain life-oriented. Like everyone in the BLS, the first thing the adolescent needs is a safe sanctuary — some space of his own where he feels safe and free from harassment or pressure from the world. He needs to have around him those things that give him comfort.

He needs to have a sense of belonging, a sense that he is a valued member of his family and his community. He needs to feel an emotional connection to others. And a sense that his life has meaning for him and for others. He needs continuity; no unnecessary life disruptions should be sprung on him. If sudden change is thrust upon the family, he needs to be brought into the process of adjustment at the earliest possible moment, given a voice and allowed to play a part in planning how to best deal with the changes.

When disaster strikes a family, parents may try to withhold information from their child in their attempts to shield him from its impact. This can easily backfire, because the child will surely pick up the vibrations of the disaster, and without concrete information, his imagination will create dire scenarios that may be worse than the actual circumstance. What's more, he will feel quite isolated with his worries, unable to seek reassurance from his parents, since the subject has been made taboo. It's okay for a child to see that life sometimes presents serious problems, and that his parents don't have all the answers. It's more important that he be shown that they have the will to search for answers, and that they want to include him in that process.

Since isolation is one of the most problematic symptoms of the Between Lives State — always one of the givens in an active suicidal crisis — an adolescent needs to feel that he is vitally connected to every possible facet of life available to him.

Meaningful volunteer work that he values and enjoys, and for which he receives positive feedback and a sense of fulfillment, can provide community connection, life meaning, and emotional connection to others, along with a sense of belonging, a feeling that the world needs and values him. We, as a society, need to rethink our parenting strategies, our school's role in their lives, and our community's responsibility to these undervalued citizens.

We as parents and as a society must become sensitized to the stressful lives most teenagers are living today; we must really listen to them and make a meaningful connection. It doesn't take a lot of time. It takes recognition of what's really important, and what is not. It helps to look back at our own adolescence and think what sort of moral support we would have appreciated having. That's what the teenagers in our lives need, too. Giving teenagers our encouragement, support and the benefit of our mature perspective will go a long way toward making their trek through the "valley of shadows of adolescence" a much easier and safer trip. It will help them enter their adult lives as more stable, forward-looking people, unencumbered by too much unfinished business from a traumatic adolescence.

8

Helping Someone through a Suicidal Crisis

In my thirty-five years as a psychotherapist it has been my privilege to support dozens of people through their suicidal crises. While it requires energy, concentration, time, and patience on my part, it has never once depressed me. On the contrary, it has instilled in me a profound respect for our human nature and our ability to survive. And it has taught me incredible things about our resilient and resourceful human consciousness. It has also made me a believer in the phenomenon of enchantments. I have never met a suicidal person who was not caught up in a temporary but scary enchantment, unable to see that other solutions to his or her problems may exist.

The Black Sludge Factor

When someone makes it known to me that he is considering suicide, I know that I am being confronted with a soul who, if he could, would say:

"My heart feels such a deep level of despair; I can't find the will to dig my way out. My every emotion is drowning in a black sludge of despair. This black sludge has become, terrifyingly, my only reality. The most optimistic thought, filtered through this black sludge, becomes black sludge also. The memories of happier times are drained of happiness and lose all meaning; past successes lose all meaning, sinking into the black sludge. Any possible future can only be seen as too meaningless to face, and also covered with black sludge. Life itself has been drained of all meaning. Any effort to find meaning in anything is immediately swallowed up by the black sludge.

"Every effort of others to try to cheer me up drives me deeper and deeper into the black sludge. The wonderful things about life that they suggest that I think about immediately become covered with the sticky black goo, but they are oblivious of this, reinforcing my feelings of being entirely alone. Their determined effort to avoid validating my black sludge reality throws me into a terrifying isolation where I am at the mercy of the black sludge that only I can see. It is the stuff of horror movies! I long for oblivion, the only escape from the black sludge.

"Worldly demands are pushing me, demanding that I 'snap out of it' and take actions to stand up against aversive worldly circumstances, as if I had herculean energies, as if I had the heart for it all. I look inside myself for some corner that is not consumed by the black sludge, some way to screw up the energy to enter the worldly fray. But I find only creeping black sludge, and it seems to mock me. The only inner encouragement I can find comes from the black sludge itself. The black sludge offers the encouragement to take some action that is compatible with black sludge. It mockingly offers me a solution that is the essence of the black sludge: death.

"And I don't even have the energy for that. Perhaps the worldly demand will push me so much that I finally galvanize my energies enough to take the black sludge solution. Perhaps the person inside who has been resisting my black sludge reality is now becoming hostile to me and will give me a push. It seems to me that the black sludge is encouraging him to push my head under."

As Freud might ask, "What do these people want?" Most of us, at some time in our life, have fallen into the pit of despair. Some have lingered there for some time. I, for one, have set up a laboratory there to do research on the subject of black sludge, enchantments, and pits of despair. One thing I know for sure is that the person covered with black sludge is in no condition to know what he wants, much less tell Freud or anyone else.

But if he has presented himself to me, I know what he wants from me. He wants immediate relief from his agony, the agony of being isolated and at the mercy of his current enchantment. So the first thing I do is end his isolation. I wade right into the sludge — I know it well, and I know that neither his enchantment nor his sludge have any power over me, that there is nothing for me to fear. I treat his sludge as just a decoration in his enchanted sludge-room. I clear off a sludgy chair and have a seat, commiserating with him about how black and bleak today's sludge seems. When he acts surprised at my comfort with his sludgy environment, I reassure him by saying, "Oh, I've been here so long, I've hung curtains." Amazingly, he smiles, something he probably hasn't done in a while. But then, a person enchanted with absolute isolation experiences a shock when someone enters his enchantment by validating his sludge reality. It's hard to keep an enchantment going when someone else willingly enters the room.

But while I may take life lightly, I never treat him or his feelings of despair lightly. My heart fills with compassion for the suffering that I know he is enduring. If he'll let me, I'll hold his hand, hug him — I would probably put him on my lap and rock him, if he'd let me! Compassionate touch is magic here. No enchantment can withstand it for long.

I remember one case where a fellow walked a long way through the snow to get to my home in Chapel Hill because the roads were impassable. Someone had given him my name as a person who was willing to deal with people's suicidal feelings. After hugging him at the door, I made him take his wet shoes off, and we sat on the couch, his feet propped up to dry his socks out. Wanting to maintain physical contact if possible, I took hold of his foot. He did not draw away, so I held onto it throughout the entire session. All through our visit, I could feel the warmth of this connection and could see a gradual draining of tension from his body. But I'm always cautious here, because he may not be able to bear touch yet. And my efforts to connect may drive him further into isolation, if he must pull away.

The most important word to remember here is respect. I respect this person caught in an enchantment as someone who is doing "universal work" for all of us. The Ancient Mysteries teach that we are all in this together, and when one person works on despair and overcomes it, it makes it possible for all of us who follow to overcome it more easily. Thus, universal work is a sort of "reprogramming" of the collective consciousness that we share. As he does his work, I see my job as assistant to him, especially in his efforts in the overcoming phase. So I sit with him and his sludgy despair. And as I tell him what I know about the subject, his feelings of isolation slowly subside. Soon, the feeling that we are taking a coffee-break from the melodrama tends to lessen the sense of urgency to take desperate actions. It's easy to see the tension ratcheting downward. Laughter enters the conversation, and, eventually, yawns. Melodrama is very tiring, and this is the first time he's relaxed in hours. Slowly but surely, our conversation infuses his consciousness with the feeling that life, with its melodramas, is a subject that can be taken a bit more lightly, and that we can make plans to give ourselves a treat later, after the disaster comes and goes. We are all in this strange, tragi-comic condition together, and it's our job to be there for each other, to share the suffering, the absurdities, and the humor involved along the way. Companions. No enchantment can withstand the light of human compassion for long. In fact, it can't withstand a visitor! And the wonderful thing about enchantment-sludge is that, with the awakening from the dream, the sludge magically disappears. Doesn't even have to be cleaned up!

Intuiting a Suicidal Crisis

When we come to understand the Between Lives State, it is relatively easy to predict the probability of someone's vulnerability to occasional, "casual" suicidal feelings, and also whether or not he's been pushed to the point of an active suicidal crisis. A rundown of current events in his life, along with any major life changes that could precipitate the loss of his world-connected ego-identity, will give us the information we need for a risk assessment. The changes we must look for are: the loss of a significant relationship, the loss of a child, the loss of a career, a promotion, a firing, a retirement, loss of a familiar environment — through natural disaster or through voluntary relocation — a return to or recent graduation from school, the completion of a major, life absorbing project, the loss of bodily function(s), loss of status, loss of a familiar life, or the loss of a major valued dream or expectation. As you can see, even the so-called "good" events of life can throw us into this ego-less state. These are the sorts of events that can take away the ego-identity that defined a person to himself in his world, catapulting him into the BLS, making him vulnerable to all its symptoms.

The Pressure Factor

Being unplugged from his energy source, his lack of energy and sense of purpose can make all of life's demands feel like just too much pressure on him, and he can be vulnerable to intermittent low-grade suicidal feelings. Less a thought than a feeling, it's a gut-level desire to just give up. However, he can drag through the days on automatic pilot for a very long time, relying on habit, as long as life makes no demands beyond the normal routine.

Precipitating Factors

Events that can push such a Between Lives person into an active suicidal crisis can be recognized, as well, because those events involve such a person in what seems to him a life crisis of some immediate, unavoidable, overwhelming worldly requirement that must be met, with seemingly no escape possible, the sort of noxious demands that cause some level of stress even for those fully connected to life, such as an impending audit by the IRS. The ego-detached person feels the pressure of this requirement bearing down relentlessly upon him and he simply hasn't the energy, motivation, nor — more significantly, the needed ego-integration — to respond to the unavoidable worldly demand. It's this demand-generated pressure that most often creates an active suicidal crisis. "Why doesn't he just go for help?" you may ask. The answer to that is: If he had the ego-integration necessary to think up that solution, he wouldn't be having trouble handling the crisis in the first place. With his current condition of ego-disintegration (he's in the raw scrambled eggs stage of the chrysalis state) he really can't think lucidly, nor see either the crisis or options clearly. In fact, given his lack of perspective, he may have an exceedingly warped view of the crisis. Keep in mind that this condition can happen to rocket scientists, ministers, professors, physicians, psychiatrists, as well as to all the rest of us. It's not a matter of being mentally deficient. It's a matter of being non-functional at the moment. The greatest electronic computer in the world can only just sit there dumbly when not plugged into its energy source. This goes for us humans, too, when our ego-identity becomes unplugged from our worldly life.

In a crisis, with seemingly no way to escape, and with an inner imperative demanding some kind of action, he may feel he has to resort to the tragically maladaptive coping strategy of suicide, as a "necessary" problem-solving solution. It's important to realize that no one truly wants to commit suicide. The ambivalence that suicidal people experience is found in their vacillation between wanting to live and feeling that they cannot. This dilemma is a source of intense suffering.

Respecting the Boundaries of a Suicidal Person

Contrary to common practice, I never ask anyone if he's having suicidal feelings, nor if he's considering suicide. This, I believe, is a violation of his boundaries and — contrary to common belief — has the potential to cause serious problems. My experience has led me to believe that if a suicidal person feels he must admit to these thoughts, feelings, and/or plans before he feels safety and trust have been established with the questioner — especially in a world that still stigmatizes a suicidal person — it tends to make him feel weaker, even mentally ill, and definitely more vulnerable. If, on the other hand, he feels he must protect himself by lying to the questioner and saying he's not considering suicide, this intensifies a suicidal person's feelings of isolation, one of the most serious — and dangerous — afflictions of an active suicidal crisis. The worst thing we can do to an actively suicidal person is intensify his sense of isolation.

Given the history of well-intentioned harassment and inadvertent abuse of suicidal people, it may sometimes be too risky to admit to having suicidal feelings, for the questioner may not be capable of handling a suicidal person's present-moment feelings. He may, instead, become enchanted with that possible future act of suicide, initiating a melodrama that quickly escalates into a series of painful, even toxic miscommunications. If a suicidal person suspects that the questioner can't handle his pain and confusion with compassion rather than fear, he may need to respond to the questioner by saying, "I'm not comfortable with your question. I don't feel we've established the necessary level of trust to discuss such a subject." The would-be helper must then either develop that trust or refer him to someone else who would be able and willing to do so. A self-test of a would-be helper is to ask oneself the question, "Am I likely to become impatient or angry at this person if he says he is suicidal?" If the answer to that question is yes, then one should recuse oneself and refer the suffering person to someone else, in order to do no harm.

Not asking the question sounds like heresy to those advocating a policy of always asking the question. But your purpose here is, not to leap into a future suicidal rescue mode, but to be present in this moment with a severely suffering person, and this very act of sharing the present moment can make a future rescue unnecessary in most cases. When the information contained here is understood, it is possible to recognize the factors that can evoke suicidal feelings and an active suicidal crisis, by asking for information that will reveal where the person is in his life transitions and, therefore, whether or not he is likely between lives.

When I determine that several Between Lives factors are present in a person's life, and that he may be currently vulnerable to the BLS symptoms, I share that information with him and mention that it's not unusual for people to experience forty uncomfortable symptoms, including suicidal feelings, under such circumstances. This accomplishes several things. It gives him information that he might relate to and be able to use to better understand his situation. It deliberately avoids invasive questions. It respects his boundaries, and that respect strengthens him. Hearing this information can make him feel more normal, and that feeling strengthens him. It also shows him that I may be a safe person to talk to about any such painful feelings, and if that's the case it helps end his isolation. And it gives him the opportunity to speak about his feelings if he needs to, without feeling that such an admission will be used against him or make him vulnerable to harassment by a rescuer. He chooses whether or not to accept the invitation to share his feelings, according to his own comfort level. And because I've proven myself to be a safe, respectful, and compassionate person who will not violate his autonomy, it helps to build the trust needed in our relationship for him to open himself to my help. It also takes such feelings out of the realm of melodrama, for I've spoken matter-of-factly about them as just another of those painful, confusing symptoms found between lives. And indeed, my thirty-five years' research has convinced me that this is what they are.

On one occasion, when I had informed a new client, a man in his mid-sixties, that suicidal feelings were a common symptom of the Between Lives State, he was quiet for a moment, and then volunteered the information that he had put a gun to his head just a few nights before. I responded to that admission with heartfelt sympathy, "I know how agonizing it is to get to that level of despair," I said. "Those are the most painful feelings a human ever experiences. It's a miracle that we have the strength to endure them. We humans are so much stronger than we realize." Tears came to his eyes and some of the tension seemed to leave his rigid body. I took his hand and he squeezed mine for a long moment.

I spoke of the irony that such weird and painful feelings could ever be considered "normal" for us to experience at times. They don't feel normal, as we've come to understand that word. But then, neither does it seem normal to be living several lifetimes in one. We went on to discuss his particular life circumstances. What he reported helped me determine that he was, indeed, between lives. I shared my perceptions with him. He agreed that this felt accurate to him. He felt like he was in a non-living state at the moment. He seemed relieved to have a label he could put on his condition and that the label wasn't related to insanity. His body relaxed perceptibly and he smiled for the first time since arriving.

Risk Assessment

My need then was to determine whether or not he was currently at risk for an immediate active suicidal crisis. He didn't know it, but I then proceeded to do a risk assessment of his current condition throughout the course of our discussion of ways to take care of ourselves while in the Between Lives State, so that we don't ever get to the active suicidal crisis stage. He reported that the precipitating crisis that had led him to put a gun to his head had been resolved: he had called his daughter, who planned to come visit him the following weekend, and in a month's time he'd be flying to the West coast to visit his son. He also reported plans he had made to spend Thanksgiving with his family. These future nurturing events actually connected him to life now, through his imagination — the crucial mental faculty that we must control to protect ourselves when we are between lives.

This gave me the information I needed to determine that the crisis that had caused him to become actively suicidal was over. Additionally, his temporary connections to life made him no longer vulnerable to an immediate return to active suicidal status. The plans he had made with his family were a firm connection to life once again, at least for now and the near future. He was no longer isolated — one of the strongest risk factors of a suicidal crisis. He also had world-connected plans that were nurturing, and no aversive demands were being made on him at the moment.

Positive Feedback

I again shared my perceptions with him and commended him for taking all the appropriate steps to prevent a replay of the miserable feelings involved in an active suicidal crisis; first, by reconnecting with nurturing family members and second, by seeking out ongoing support. He agreed that he no longer felt that he was in crisis and believed that this new information about his Between Lives status gave him the needed perspective to prevent any future crises, to that degree, from occurring.

I believe that my respecting him as a healthy person in spite of his recent suicidal crisis was important in restoring his confidence in himself and in his sanity. By giving him a rational perspective about his condition and pronouncing it "normal" for those life conditions, I enabled him to feel normal again. This is crucial to the return of an emotionally healthy mental state in which he could feel in charge of himself and his life again, ending any chance of his getting caught up in another confusing suicidal enchantment — at least for now.

Providing a Lifeline

Since his ongoing BLS status meant that any new aversive worldly demand could precipitate a new active crisis, I gave him my phone number and invited him to call me for an "instant support group meeting," should any new crisis appear on the horizon, so that we could "nip it in the bud." I informed him that he was to treat the phone call to me like a prescription, to be used as needed. This lifeline would hopefully prevent feelings of isolation from returning, once he left my presence. Had I determined that he was, in fact, in an active suicidal crisis, I would have worked with him until I was assured that the crisis had abated, keeping in mind the following considerations and techniques.

Thirty Facts to Consider about Suicidal Feelings

- No one wants to commit suicide. As mentioned about, the ambivalence that suicidal people experience is a vacillation between wanting to live and feeling that they cannot. This dilemma is a source of intense suffering.
- Not everyone with suicidal feelings is in an active suicidal crisis. Crisis status should not be a requirement for giving compassionate attention to a person experiencing these painful feelings.
- Not everyone in active suicidal crisis takes his life at this time, during this crisis. But the way he's treated when he reaches out for help this time will determine how — or if — he reaches out for help if there is a next time.
- Everyone who does take his own life does so as a direct result of his suicidal feelings. We need to understand these feelings and deal with their cause, to prevent the escalation of such feelings into an active suicidal crisis.
- Suicidal feelings, in and of themselves, are a valid emotional condition of the present moment, deserving our respectful attention and compassion, free from any fears or requirements on our part about any possible future actions of the suffering person. The validity of their feelings does not depend on whether or not the person is likely to act upon them. These feelings deserve our attention because they are causing the person much confusion, pain, and suffering now.
- Suicidal feelings are a complex convolution of confusing, painful thoughts, beliefs, feelings, and pressures — a hopeless tangle. A suicidal person has wrestled with his tangle of confused and painful thoughts and feelings until he becomes a prisoner of the tangle. Suicidal feelings are

the most painful combination of thoughts and emotions that a human can ever experience — they can be agony.

- It is the agony that causes a suicidal person to reach out desperately for relief through some kind of human contact. He reaches out with the only energy that is still free of the tangle. It may not be his most attractive or lucid energy.

- He may be filled with anger, which comes from his perception of being powerless concerning circumstances where he needs his power. He may feel outraged that, according to his perceptions, circumstances leave him no choice but to take his own life. If you would be of help, don't be turned off by his anger. Anger may be his only strength at the moment. Don't let it push your buttons. But don't argue with his anger either. No one wants to lose an argument. But if he wins, he'll have won the argument to kill himself.

- If you feel that he is "threatening" to commit suicide unless you come up with a rescue, you can stay out of potentially dangerous games by saying with heartfelt compassion, "I'm aware of how powerless I am over any future actions of yours, so I won't go there. But I am willing to be with you now and deal with you and with your life and your distress."

This will short-circuit the frustrating and potentially dangerous game that many would-be rescuers find themselves in when they become entangled in their own emotions of fear, responsibility, helplessness, blame, and finally, frustrated anger of their own, against this suicidal person whom they perceive to be snaring them into a dangerous, no-win rescue game.

- Healing a suicidal crisis never requires a rescuer to wrestle with possible future actions of the suicidal person. I repeat, never. Becoming preoccupied with the possible future actions of the suicidal person prevents you from "being present" with his present-moment agony and isolation.
- If you become enchanted with that possible future suicide, the suffering person feels unheard and unseen, increasing his painful feelings of isolation. He may perceive your struggle to control his future actions as just more pressure and harassment. He may feel he must convince you that he isn't feeling suicidal after all, lest you "turn him in to the authorities." But this charade drains him more, and makes him regret ever reaching out for relief from isolation. And his suicidal feelings may escalate.
- Remember that the very effort he has made for contact is a step he has already taken out of his isolation and toward life. Don't push him back into crisis with your fears. Instead, welcome him to your presence as a sanctuary and a pressure-free Time Out space from the melodrama.
- Dealing with a suicidal crisis is similar to dealing with an over-heated pressure cooker. You remove the overheated kettle from the source of heat and open a safety-valve, inviting the steam to safely escape while you stand by — not alarming yourself by the sight and sound of the steam, because you know that its release is preventing an explosion. You merely provide it with an unpressured environment for cooling down.
- You don't risk an explosion by opening the pressure cooker while the pressure is still on. A similar explosion can happen to a suicidal person if he is pressured too soon with probing questions, confrontations, exhortations, or

solutions. Cool it. Allow ventilation. Just stand by and be respectfully, compassionately cool.

- Physical contact is the quickest means of relieving the pressure and the isolation felt by a suicidal person. Compassionate physical touch — holding his hand, for instance — is a direct message to his heart of connection, of caring, of comfort, if he can bear to be touched.
- Empathy is a healing balm to a suicidal person. It helps to end the isolation. It lances the painful boil, releasing the unbearable inner toxic pressures, bringing instant relief.
- A suicidal person is already overloaded with thoughts. Having to process too many words from a would-be helper can add more pressure. Let your approach be a quiet, slow-moving, respectful one.
- Don't rub salt in his wounds by exhorting the sufferer with how wonderful life is. Either his life is not so wonderful at the moment, or else he knows it's wonderful but believes that he's not allowed by circumstances to live it any more. Some suicidal persons are experiencing an emotional nausea toward life. You wouldn't rave about food to a physically nauseated person.
- There are identifiable conditions and circumstances that make suicidal feelings seem logical to the mind of a suicidal person. These conditions and circumstances are part of the Between Lives transitions of normal life, and with a supportive environment can be traversed safely. But going through these transition periods is similar to walking a tightrope over an abyss with no visible goal on the other side to focus one's vision on for keeping one's balance.

- A suicidal person is like a tightrope walker who doesn't want to jump, but feels he has to jump, because otherwise he's going to fall. Such tightrope walking need not be labeled "sick" in order to be recognized as dangerous. The great need at such moments is for a Time Out platform. You as a compassionate friend can furnish safe Time Out space by "being there" for the tightrope walker with your quiet presence, compassion, and confidence, without putting more pressure on him. You can readily understand that it would not be helpful to argue fearfully with such a precariously balanced tightrope walker about not jumping or falling — nor would it be helpful if your thoughts were consumed with the fear that he might fall on you.
- Remember that just staying with him, keeping him company, can be all that's required to break the enchantment and make him feel normal again. And remember this: Time is on your side. Active suicidal crises are feverish enchantments that tend to run their course and then subside.
- Don't ever become enchanted with the belief that you are a suicidal person's last resort. Trust and respect his cosmic connection to the universe. Stay out of the potentially dangerous enchantment of the rescue game.
- Be aware of your own current limitations when confronted by a suicidal person. If you don't feel capable at the moment of handling his crisis, don't hesitate to tell him of your limitation. Rather, refer him to some person or some agency that could help. Explain that you currently can't deal with his situation as helpfully as he deserves, and you don't want to cause him more pain by any well-meant ineptitude on your part. Tell him that you will hold

him in your heart and your prayers as he does his work because you know that we are all in this together. The best help you can give anyone, anyway, is moral and spiritual support. Ask if there is some other friend whom he would find supportive that you can call for him.

- If nothing seems to be working and the feverish active suicidal crisis doesn't seem to subside, suggest that Time Out hospitalization might be a loving thing he could do for himself. Ask if he'd like for you to help arrange that. Assure him that he'd be able to check himself out in 48 hours if he wishes to.

- If he wants additional help, call the National Suicide Prevention Hotline (1-800-273-8255 at the time of this writing) or text the Crisis Text Line (text HOME to 741741).

- If he doesn't want additional help, but you do, tell him that you need help, and call for advice, if you feel the need.

- When the crisis is over, talk over options for handling the pressing problems that precipitated the crisis in the first place. Be sure he has a sensible plan for dealing with the problems before you let him go. Tell him that your concern is that you don't want him to go through so much pain over this issue again.

- Invite him to call if he needs to connect again. This invitation will give him an ongoing connection that can help prevent isolation from returning. Even though he's not likely to call, just knowing that he can helps him to maintain his regained poise, and prevents him from falling back into the enchantment once he's left your presence.

- Before you part company, make sure he has a date for some nurturing, life-connecting activity in the next few days. This gives him a grounding connection to ongoing life.
- Having an understanding of the life-conditions that can place a person at risk for experiencing suicidal feelings can enable you to be a part of the supportive environment needed by all of us when crossing the abysses in life. It can help you to cross those inevitable abysses more easily yourself, when they present themselves to you as the path you must take to your next life.

9

Helping Yourself through a Suicidal Crisis When No Other Help is at Hand

On those rare occasions when a suicidal crisis arises, we're not likely to be sitting conveniently in the presence of our most nurturing friend. A sense of isolation is almost always involved with such a crisis. Therefore, we would be wise to have a plan for taking care of ourselves if we're alone in such a dire situation. The following strategies for just such an emergency were originally written for a friend who had called me from Seattle during a suicidal crisis. We talked for a long time, till the sense of crisis had diminished and we were finally laughing. I promised to send him a list of strategies to have on hand for future reference in the likely event of another crisis, for he was clearly between lives, having lost his most recent life-connected ego-identity through divorce, and under pressure from difficult life circumstances. That's the usual set-up for suicidal crises. If the following suggestions don't fit your needs, they may at least help you get clear about what you would need, to get you through such a crisis as safely and swiftly as possible with as little suffering as possible.

Emergency Mode

When severe suicidal feelings or despair wash over you, consider them just symptoms (like severe nausea is just a symptom of seasickness) and click into a pre-planned Emergency Mode that you have prepared in advance, such as the following:

- Find a sanctuary in your mind and stay there. To be mentally healthy, we all would be wise to have an imaginary sanctuary, prepared and used by us during normal everyday meditation times. A sacred space to which we can retreat where no stress can touch us. I enjoy mentally visiting my grandparent's citrus farm, where I know every orange tree and rose bush growing there. It's a place where nothing of the world can disturb my peace of mind. It's a place I can retreat to at a moment's notice, whenever worldly pressures overwhelm me. It's a great Time Out place for me when I'm overloaded with stress, and a safe sanctuary, should I feel suicidal while in the Between Lives State.

- Suspend any decision-making indefinitely. When we feel suicidal, our overheated coping system is not capable of making good or rational decisions. But we often don't have enough perspective to realize that a decision can and should be postponed. A friend who sometimes suffered from severe PMS symptoms told me that whenever she feels strongly that a decision must be made Right Now!, she has a rule that she must postpone that decision for three days. "Too many times I've been fooled by my overreacting mind into making a crisis out of something undeserving of crisis status, and into making rash and foolish decisions that my normal self would not have made three days later," she explained. This is equally true when we're feeling desperate enough to consider suicide as one of our options. That should be a clue that we're not capable at the moment of making wise decisions and should postpone any decision for the duration of this emotional state.

- If some particular decision must be made immediately, write down the options and just choose the easiest (suicide does not qualify). Forget the complications involved. It need not be the perfect decision, or even a permanent one. These aspects are not important just now. Surviving is what's important.
- Treat your thoughts and feelings like so many inner children. You may not know what to do with grief, but you do know a grief-stricken child must be comforted. You may be confused by a sick thought, but you would put a sick child to bed and take measures to nurture it, meanwhile disregarding its delirious ramblings.
- Keep inner children in the playpen of the Present Moment. Concentrate on taking care of yourself one moment at a time. Thoughts about the future are not allowed right now. All you have to deal with is surviving the Present Moment.
- Strictly guard the use of the imagination. Shut it down for now. Tell your inner kids firmly: "The Imagination is not a toy!"
- Forbid your mind from tormenting your heart with despairing thoughts. Just as you would stop a child from tormenting his nauseated sibling with sickening imaginings, so you must stop your mind from coloring your world with grim and hopeless images.

- This is not the time to survey your problems in the name of problem-solving. Keep bringing the straying mind back to the tasks of the Present Moment: Safety, Comfort, Surviving.
- Do not allow yourself the luxury of asking why you should survive. Just survive.
- Use all healthy means available to comfort yourself. (Avoid attempts to drown your sorrow in alcohol. There is ample evidence that sorrow knows how to swim.)

Three of the most comforting things to do at such a time are:

- Sleep: Sleep as much as you wish to and can. It's very healing and does no harm. Give yourself permission to curl up under the covers in the fetal position and stay there for as long as you wish.
- Get a Massage. Go to a professional masseuse if possible for a massage. If no one is available, give yourself a hand and foot massage. Massage your face and neck. Massage each finger. Massage the skin between thumb and forefinger, which is a pressure point for relieving stress.
- Tap Inner spiritual resources: A Christian friend told me, "Once when I was experiencing unbearable grief and pressure from a tragic situation in my life, I remembered Jesus's promise to send us the Holy Comforter. So I implored the Holy Comforter, if he could hear me, to please comfort me. I was astonished by the instant feeling of enfoldment in a soothing, comforting energy!" she said. "While nothing outwardly seemed changed, I felt so comforted that, after resting in that energy for a time, I was able to return to the outer problem feeling stronger, more centered and able to deal with it."

All religions of the world have a spiritual comforter available to believers, ready to comfort when asked. Use this resource. If there are circumstances that make you feel that you do not deserve to be comforted, you must by-pass the outer realm of personality and go to a deeper level, to the level of your soul where we are all made of the same sacred spiritual stuff. This aspect of you is connected to God and free of fault. Cling to that inner sacred self. Allow it to comfort your outer self as it would a transgressing child whom it loves unconditionally, despite its transgressions. If that feels impossible to do at the moment, then just comfort yourself because it's part of the prescription of the Emergency Mode.

- Since your judgment is malfunctional during suicidal crises, suspend self-judgment for now. If you were dealing with acute symptoms of stage fright, it would be counter-productive to critique your flaws as a public speaker at that time, as that would only increase your stage fright. Similarly, in comforting yourself when feeling suicidal, refuse to entertain critical, judgmental thoughts about yourself.

- Face the unavoidable with nonresistance. If the aversive circumstance that triggered the suicidal crisis is bearing down upon you relentlessly, forcing your hand, remember the words of Isaiah: "In quietness and in confidence shall be my strength," and instead of pursuing escape as the only solution, simply turn quietly, and face the disaster without resistance. Let it wash over you, let the worst happen, and do not be moved. Play your part in the scene, but refuse to participate in the melodrama of it. Remain detached. And when the scene has played itself out, quietly pick yourself up and move on. There is immense strength in nonresistance.

- If someone exhorts you to work on your problems right now, order them to back off. When a crash victim is being disentangled from a tree limb, the rescue workers do not exhort him to confront his accident-prone behaviors. That's not the appropriate time, and they are not the appropriate facilitators of that kind of behavioral work.
- Surviving the present moment is your only work right now. This is not the time or place for confronting your inner or outer problems. You will choose the time and the acceptable facilitator some time in that future that you are not allowing yourself to think about at the moment. Right now, you are working hard, disciplining yourself to stay in the present moment, and protecting/nurturing your inner children. Waste no energy on anything else.
- Do not, in your confused state, invite persecution. Don't expose your vulnerability to anyone who cannot be trusted to be supportive of you right now. People who mean well can, in their ignorance, be hurtful, even toxic.
- Do not set yourself up for a letdown. Don't phone someone if a possible negative response or a busy signal could devastate you.
- Consider reaching out for help. A suicidal crisis is like an over-heated pressure cooker. Given a cooling-off period, most such crises dissipate within a few minutes, a few hours at most. In that rare instance when the feverish energy seems to keep on and on, consider reaching out for help.
- Call 911 or the National Suicide Prevention Hotline (1-800-273-8255 at the time of this writing) or text the Crisis Text Line (text HOME to 741741) any time of the day or night. Tell them you want to consider a possible Time Out

hospitalization for stabilizing a suicidal crisis. They'll handle the rest. If you wish, they'll even send someone to pick you up and transport you to the hospital. You will not be surrendering your power to anyone because, by law, you may check yourself out of the hospital — after forty-eight hours, usually — when you feel better. This is a very loving thing to do for yourself.

- Finally, endure. We're all in this tragi-comedy we call life together. I suspect that we are each a unique viewpoint of God, all equally important in the cosmic scheme of things.

- Consider this to be a prescription, one that you can use in the future, should the blessings of long life, spiritual growth, and the mystical process of transformation take you again to the edge of the abyss.

10

How to Live Multiple Lives Without the Trauma of the BLS

Given what we now understand about the Between Lives State, how can we enjoy this blessing of multiple lives lived out in one lifetime, without suffering the downside of the BLS? Are there things we can do in our present life to soften the effects of that inevitable transformational process that occurs when our ego-identity expires but we don't? If we recognize, even as we begin a new ego-life, that its end will eventually come, can we then live that life in such a way that our next one will be enhanced without taking anything from our current commitments? What can we do now to make future transitions relatively trauma free?

I asked the people in my Life Transitions groups what they would do differently, knowing what they now know about the Between Lives phenomenon. We came up with some proactive steps we can all take toward a possible future life even while fully living out our current one. The following are some suggested strategies.

Have realistic expectations. We need to expect the day will come when our parenting role is no longer needed, when retirement or downsizing could eliminate our position at work, when a long-term relationship will end, when an all-consuming project will be finished, when the vicissitudes of the aging process could bring life-changing limitations.

Don't fall into an enchantment. Being wholly in the present moment is, indeed, an excellent way to get the most from life. But not if it becomes an enchantment whereby we are shocked when a major phase of our life ends. First, we must recognize that in the material world everything is temporary. Our philosophy of appreciating life in the present moment must be informed by the knowledge that, nevertheless, this too shall pass.

Empty-nester Katherine spoke about her years of raising children:

> "I suppose I knew, in theory, that someday my life as an active parent would come to an end. After all, no children ever stay stuck in childhood forever. But I gave it little thought. I was so completely immersed in my busy, hectic job — as household manager, purchasing agent, appointment secretary, chauffeur, school consultant, nurse, not to mention chief cook and bottle washer — that I never gave much thought to the future, except to think that it would be nice to someday have a moment to myself. I never realized that after this 'feast' of activity would be the inevitable famine. And the things that I did for my family held a lot of meaning for me. My multi-faceted role seemed necessary to the successful functioning of our family. My activities kept the family healthy and happy. I valued myself in my role, and didn't foresee a day when it would have no value at all."

Don't put all your eggs in one basket

"What would I do differently, if I had it to do over again?" Katherine continued.

"Given what I know now about the inherent limitations of my ego-identity as a parent, I think I would spend more time developing my interests, expanding my world beyond my family. For instance, I wish I had enrolled in school myself as soon as my youngest child started school. I could have taken a couple of college courses at a time during the kids' school hours, pursuing whatever interested me. This could have been one of my hobbies. It would have gotten me out into the world meeting people, discussing stimulating ideas, gaining a broader perspective about life. And it would have been a way to do a long-term feasibility study about which direction I'd like to take in my 'next life' when my hands-on parenting role ended.

"I would still do my job at home and be there when the kids were home, but I'd never again lose myself totally in a role that is fated to end absolutely. One of the most important things an at-home parent does for her children is to just be there when they're home. But there were at least seven hours every weekday when I was home alone. I filled my days with busywork. But many of the things I did could have been done by others. Some of my time could have been spent on nurturing and developing other parts of myself. If I had it to do over again, I would spend a lot of that time on furthering my education. And I would pursue hobbies that could someday be the nucleus of a new life — like creative writing. Those years that I spent at home could have been a great gestation period for expanding my ego-identity and nurturing the beginnings of my next ego-life without cheating my family at all. It just never occurred to me to use that time in that way."

Visualize a future life. Imagine what it will be like when the end of your current life arrives. Visualize your life as if it were a play on a stage. Sit in the audience and watch the progression of events onstage as they flow beyond the events of today to their possible conclusions. As you view the ongoing play that is your life, realize that you are the playwright who must write a sequel to this play. Given what you know about yourself as the protagonist in your life-play, what sort of storyline for a sequel comes to mind as you observe yourself in this current story being enacted onstage? What are the major traits of your character that could indicate where your next life adventure will be?

Cultivate your latent personality traits. As you view yourself upon that stage in your current life-drama, study the person that you are. What are some hidden aspects of your character that are not being expressed in this current phase of your life? Are you a person who would love to be in the middle of things, organizing and coordinating other people's activities? Is there an aspect of yourself who would love to be sequestered in a library doing research on some intriguing subject? Are you fascinated by human nature? Would you love to champion some worthwhile cause?

Make a list of all such aspects of yourself that you can discern. Imagine a sequel that uses these aspects as the storyline for a possible next life-drama. Notice which ones stir up the most enthusiasm in you.

Consider what factors will make the sequel different from the play just ending. No doubt, the protagonist (you) will not be in the role of parent of small children again if that's what's ending in the current play. If you're being retired in the current play after thirty years with the same company, you'll not begin your sequel playing the part of a young person just starting out in your first job.

Get clear about your heart's values. Take along on your next vacation a good book that can help you define your values, especially those things for which you value yourself, for these are the crucial components of consciousness that give us the feeling of being alive. There are dozens of excellent self-help books out there that can help you clarify your values.

Keep a healthy perspective. Many decades ago, Joanne Woodward, who had been nominated for her first Academy Award, was interviewed while she was making the dress she planned to wear to the event. She told the interviewer that she kept reminding herself, "This, too, shall pass." Good or bad, events do pass, and new events will happen. If we are staying true to our heart's values, we will feel centered through all the outer changes that come to pass.

Don't indulge in magical wishful thinking that can't be made real in your life. If you have just turned fifty in your current play, then the sequel will have to be written for a protagonist who is fifty-plus. No amount of wishful thinking will allow the protagonist to be twenty-five again. Fortunately, in today's world, fifty-plus people can do most of the things available to those in their twenties — and, often, do them better. Make a practical list of the "givens" that must be a part of the sequel. Then determine which factors can and should be different from the current story being played out now on the stage of your life.

Remember, as you gather the information for writing your next life-play, the whole point of the sequel is to take your protagonist-self happily through interesting adventures until you reach another satisfying conclusion. And as long as you don't kill off your main character in the sequel, there's no limit to the number of sequels you may create.

Actively prepare. Start preparing now for eventually stepping out of your current role and into your next one, even while you happily live out your present one. Don't withdraw your energy from your current life. That would not be a healthy way to prepare. Living fully now is indeed the best strategy for preparing for your future life expression. And you can live more fully by developing other, dormant, aspects of yourself, which can only enrich your current life. In this way you can make the process of next-life preparation a part of your ongoing life now. Are there interesting courses you could be taking now that would be useful in your next life? Are there hobbies you'd like to pursue now that could lead to a new life later? Are there degrees you could be earning now in your spare time? Are there feasibility studies you could be doing? Do you need to be funding that future life through a savings plan now?

Invest in yourself. An older generation of women grew up hearing their parents comment that sending their daughter to college would be a poor investment since she would just marry and raise children and never use her education. Those days are gone forever. Women who spend their early adult years at home raising a family can look forward to another whole lifetime in which they can have a career after the family has flown the nest. Returning to school while your children are still living at home is an excellent investment in yourself and your future life. And you'll be a great role model for your children to emulate.

Another way to invest in yourself is to pay yourself a salary. Even fifty or a hundred dollars a month for twenty years in a money market account can provide a sizable nest-egg for seed money to invest in the start-up of your next life.

Plan your next life. Plan on the ending of your current way of life, not by planning your funeral, but by planning your next ego expression. Gerald, an engineer who was promoted out of engineering into an executive position for which he had no aptitude, was seriously shaken by the experience of climbing the ladder of success, only to discover that it led to the loss of his engineer identity, the ego-identity for which he valued himself. This made him wary of ever again letting the world dictate what "success" was for him. "I never want to let my work life get out of my control again. While retirement from the firm is still a long way off, I'm already planning for it. I want to keep using my engineering skills my entire lifetime. And there's no reason why I can't. I'm making plans to work as a consultant after I leave the firm."

Have contingency plans. "I've started writing for engineering journals," Gerald said, "as a way to develop a reputation and establish myself as a future consultant. I won't have to give up my identity as an engineer in my next life. I'm also looking into the possibility of teaching some math courses in adult education. I think I would enjoy teaching." Since we can't know the future with certainty, it's wise to have a Plan B, and maybe even a Plan C and D, in case Plans A and B can't be realized.

Cultivate social resources. Develop a support group that is independent of your daily life. I know of one group of women who have remained friends since grammar school, maintaining contact through letters, phone calls, and occasional lunches through the years. They do not include their families in their get-togethers, preferring to keep this support group separate from their personal lives. This preserves the group gatherings as a Time Out from their daily lives; it's a community of caring people who nurture and support each member when she is inevitably confronted with a major life transition such as death, divorce, or other circumstance that could catapult her into the Between Lives State.

We often neglect to cultivate our personal life in favor of our marriage, as if it's an "either/or" proposition. Spouses sometimes reinforce this tendency, expressing their dislike for any outside activities on our part that take us away from home. And since we believe strongly in nurturing our committed relationships, we often drop former friendships and interests in favor of just those that include our spouse. On the face of it, this seems harmless. But there's a better way to enrich our marriage. And that's by becoming a more well-rounded and engaging person with interests that extend beyond those that find expression in the home or with our partner.

Mary lost her whole life when she lost her husband. She spoke of how she had limited her social life during her marriage. "George had golf," she said.

"After he retired, he played golf several times a week with his golfing buddies. So he had a social life separate from me. But I never felt the need to develop an independent social life. We had our mutual friends and were very active socially with them. And when George played golf, I enjoyed puttering around the house without him following me around. I enjoyed being alone on those occasions.

"But seeing how isolated I became after he passed away, when I no longer had the social life we had previously shared with other couples, couples who now seemed uncomfortable with an unattached woman in the group, I definitely wish I had done things differently — I would involve myself in the garden club and in more church activities. If I had my old life back, I would definitely cultivate a social life of my own, as George did."

Kevin, a perennial student, spoke of how isolated his academic world was from the business community.

"If I had it to do over again, I think I wouldn't just take boring, dead-end jobs to support myself while I went to school. I would turn my need for a paycheck into feasibility studies of various types of careers, maybe working as a temp in many different jobs to see what turned me on. If I found some work that I'd like to make a career of, this would connect my school life to my life beyond graduation, ending the feeling of being isolated from real life. And after graduation, I wouldn't feel like I was being thrown out into an unfamiliar world. I would already have connections to my next life."

Cultivate spiritual resources. Carl Jung, the famous Swiss psychiatrist who spent his lifetime studying individuation and the processes of consciousness transformation, believed that most of those people who became involved with this endeavor of self-actualization had been put upon this path through some misfortune tripping them up early in life, compelling them to search for deeper answers than the surface of life provided. Adversity is often the reason we begin our search for spiritual answers. And then, long after we've put the adversity behind us, the spiritual search takes on an importance of its own, enriching our lives and facilitating our growth on many levels. We may eventually look back upon that original adversity as a blessing in disguise.

If we truly embrace the concept of living several ego-lives in the span of one physical lifetime, then we have reason enough to begin our search for the deeper meanings of life now, without waiting for some adversity to give us a wake-up call. The very thought that our current identity comes with a time limit built into it shakes up our unrealistic feelings of permanency about our apparent world. The more we can awaken ourselves to the deeper meanings of life now, the less likely we are to suffer a rude awakening sometime in the future.

Develop a cosmic view of life. To inoculate ourselves against the worst of the forty symptoms that can be stimulated in the Between Lives State, we would be wise to cultivate our cosmic connections to life. We are more than daughter or son, parent, spouse, employee, or professional. We are souls — spiritual beings. And our environment is more than home, school, or work. We live in a spiritual universe, connected to every other part of the universe, in relation to every other soul on the planet. At some point in our spiritual life journey, we realize that we are all like fingers on the same hand — individualized, but vitally connected. We discover that we truly are all in this together.

When we develop a cosmic view of life, we are more likely to maintain a healthy perspective in the Between Lives State, less likely to fall prey to the depressing imaginings and melodramatic crises that suggest themselves to us in the BLS. We are more willing to let go of that which is ending and look forward to the adventures that lie ahead. And should we suddenly find ourselves seemingly suspended on a metaphorical tightrope above an abyss, our cosmic viewpoint becomes the balancing rod that helps us keep our equilibrium and poise as we create a Time Out platform where we can find safety until we are able to move toward solid ground again and begin a new life expression.

A cosmic viewpoint enriches our lives beyond measure. Perceiving ourselves as spiritual beings living in a spiritual universe that is governed by spiritual law helps us to perceive our life as existing on a grand continuum. From this perspective, we can see the endings and new beginnings we experience as mere punctuation in the story of our individual life. At the same time we can recognize these stages as phases of a life that is greater than any of its parts. This recognition gives us the inner strength and courage to face every ending with appreciation for what was, and to anticipate every new beginning with enthusiasm.

11

Implications of My Research Findings

I think our first mistake was allowing medical professionals like Freud to define our psychological behavior. Their "medical model" viewpoint weighs behavior in terms of "sick" or "well," but these labels have little to do with either behavior or psychological phenomena. Human behavior, in general, is adaptive, aimed at adjusting to our environment, and when necessary, creating the environment we need. This ability to adjust to circumstances is the secret of humanity's successful survival over many thousands of years of environmental hardship and change.

Our problem today is that our adjustments are further complicated by our need to adapt to an ever more complex and rapidly changing world. The fact that we are living longer, healthier, richer lives, outliving our life roles several times over, pursuing several disparate careers in one lifetime, has vastly complicated our psychological and social adjustments. It is seldom clear what course we should take, or even what to think, or how to feel about the changes thrust upon us. Yet clarity is essential for making wise decisions and appropriate adjustments.

My research findings indicate that one of the greatest needs of our society today is ongoing proactive, psycho-social assistance and support — in the mode of a "wellness model" — if we are to maintain healthy communities. Such assistance and support available to every individual early on and throughout our adjustment process would strengthen our mental/emotional/social wellbeing and reduce the development of confusion, depression, substance abuse, and suicide.

The BLS is a Public Health Issue

Providing proactive professional insight, perspective, and support when we most need it could prevent the development of maladjustments, in the form of psychological and social problems later on. The medical model of our psychological nature does not serve us well here. Actually, a "horticultural model" might be more apt. To be healthy, all living organisms need the same things: a supportive environment that supplies all the "trace elements" that nurture health and happiness — nutritious food, good air, water, and a suitable climate conducive to healthy growth. We humans need all those things plus a responsive community, with institutions that are designed to address and meet our psychological and social needs. And we need these things up front, not after the deficiencies have caused us to become a "sick" organism — which is the place where our current institutions step in and go to work.

When we are between lives, our temporary loss of identity — a condition that doesn't feel temporary — and the ensuing loss of our connection to the world and to our familiar support system give us the common need for a transitions community, to end our isolation during our life transitions. A sense of isolation is the one crucial factor present in every suicidal crisis. Not everyone who feels isolated becomes suicidal, but everyone who feels suicidal does feel an acute isolation. And merely being surrounded by people doesn't faze our sense of isolation. We need people who understand and empathize with our condition during our ego-shattering transitions. We need people who are "in the same boat," because knowing others who are going through a similar transition gives us the assurance that we are not alone, that community exists for us even while we are between lives.

Needed: A New Community Paradigm

Public health institutions would be wise to establish "wellness centers" in every community for the purpose of providing, on an ongoing basis, the psychological and social "nutrients" so necessary to a healthy community. These centers would be available to support and assist us when we are in life transitions, when we are trying to understand our changing environment and our role in it. They would provide us with ongoing psychological and emotional support throughout our process of discovering and making the necessary adjustments we must make: clarifying our options, discovering how to make those adjustments in the easiest, healthiest ways possible. Proactively cultivating community health must be the focus of every public institution, if we wish to prevent the development of serious societal illnesses such as poverty, crime, drug abuse, spousal and child abuse, murder, and suicide.

Our life circumstances have profoundly changed over the past several decades. We no longer have supportive extended families, or even long-term caring neighbors, to serve as our community. This makes isolation a given in our scattered society today. Nor do we have the energy to create community for ourselves during life transitions, when we need it most. Today's fragile family is the end product of many years of "morphing," adjusting to survive in a world that is not responding realistically to what each family member, nor the family as a whole really needs. The struggle for financial survival has pushed aside the family's more basic human needs that would ensure its emotional and psychological well-being: the need for family time and family bonding, for emotional and psychological nurturing. But families can be strong and healthy again in a new way, with timely and appropriate help.

A holistic, proactive model of psycho-social help would mean that the institutions that exist to serve the public — schools, human service agencies, criminal justice systems, mental health and public health institutions — would re-form themselves to be proactively responsive to the real needs of people today.

Children need life transitions support groups within schools, to strengthen their sense of belonging to a caring community, and to help them adjust to the experiences that shatter their lives, such as divorce or family relocation. Adolescents need ongoing life transitions support groups to help them safely traverse the wide abyss between their child self and their adult identity. Life transitions support groups are needed on college campuses to help students keep perspective during this shaky ego-transformation period.

Young adults need life transitions support groups to facilitate their transition from dependent to independent life. New parents need life transitions support groups to ease their transition to a new identity and a new lifestyle. Working parents/stay-at-home parents/single parents all need support groups available to minimize their stress and isolation, and these could dramatically reduce the incidence of child abuse and neglect caused by parental overload, isolation, and desperation. If mental health and public health institutions cannot provide these services, then we must create new institutions that can, institutions that are relevant to the needs of society today.

In Summary

The recognition of the Between Lives State should change the way we view the human condition and its care, for it indicates that at least forty uncomfortable symptoms – including suicidal feelings – are predictable psychological phenomena of the BLS, and that a person between lives can be expected to need timely, thoughtful attention and support, in order to prevent the development of the more pathological symptoms. Suicide is the end product of our ignoring the BLS person until he is so tangled in the snares of the BLS that he exhibits the symptoms of mental illness. We need to view the BLS as the normal — if quirky — reaction to our temporary loss of connection to life. And our institutions of health must make available the needed psycho-social "nutrients" required by us when in life transitions.

Once we understand our psychological needs in this era of long, rich, multiple lifetimes, and the roles that our institutions must play in meeting those needs in order to maintain healthy communities, the solutions will come easily and quickly. We can speed up this process of change by advocating for the development of a wellness model of responsive community support. Then we humans can reap the benefits of traversing multiple rich lives during this *one* lifetime, and do it without really dying!